High Shelf

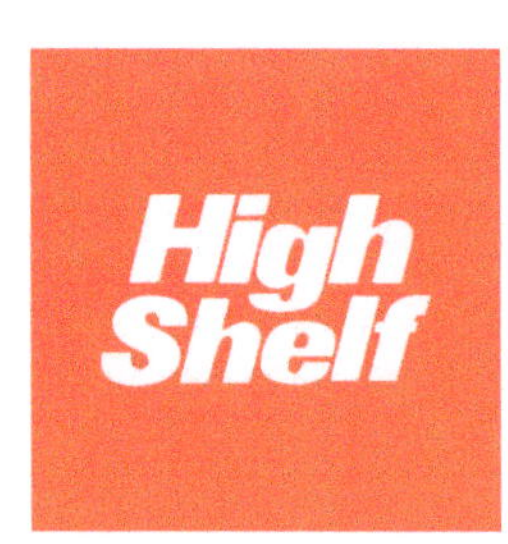

High Shelf XXXII. July 2021.
Portland, Oregon.
Copyright 2021, High Shelf Press

ISBN: 978-1-952869-36-5

Cover Image by Paula Camacho
Design, Layout and Editing by C. M. Tollefson

With special thanks to:
David Seung, Eric Hoskins, Megan Kim, & River Elizabeth Hall.

High Shelf XXXII

July 2021

"... Here: it all exists,
billows then burns..."

J.B. Fredkin

"... Time was the first ingredient.
Patience until the Earth began to
nurture its ideas into passions..."

Josalyn Switzer

Table Of Contents

Flicker

Ed McManis

Everything matters
less
than you think.

There is more
nothing
than distant starlight.

Dark Matter
is God's
backswing,

and here you wait
fumbling to light
your one candle,

trying to see
the outline
of your family

in the dark
passing the lighter,
survivors.

after midnight.

Miniature Malekpour

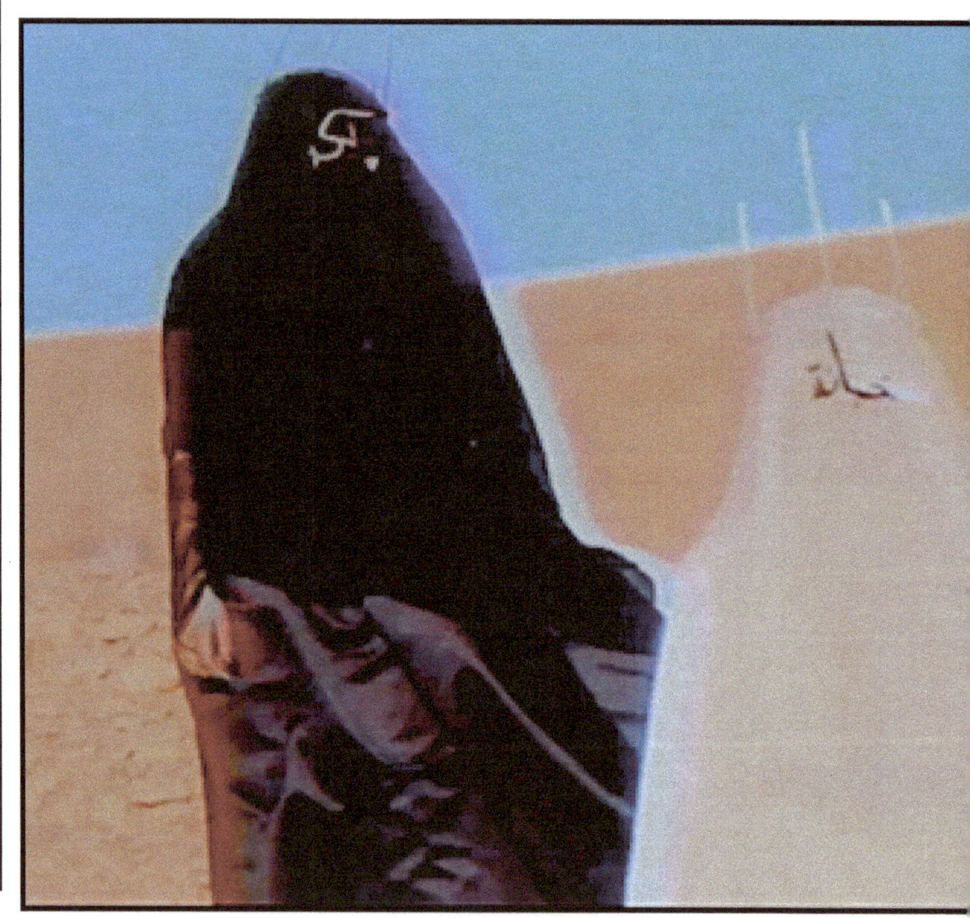

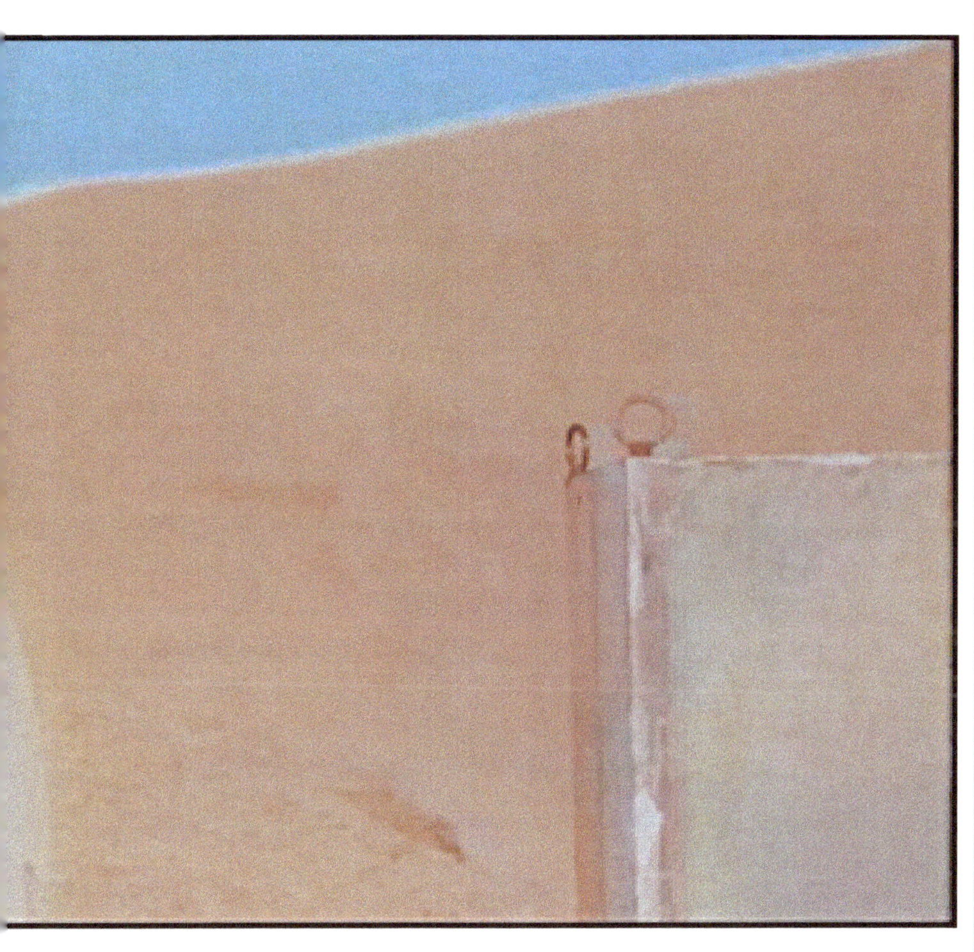

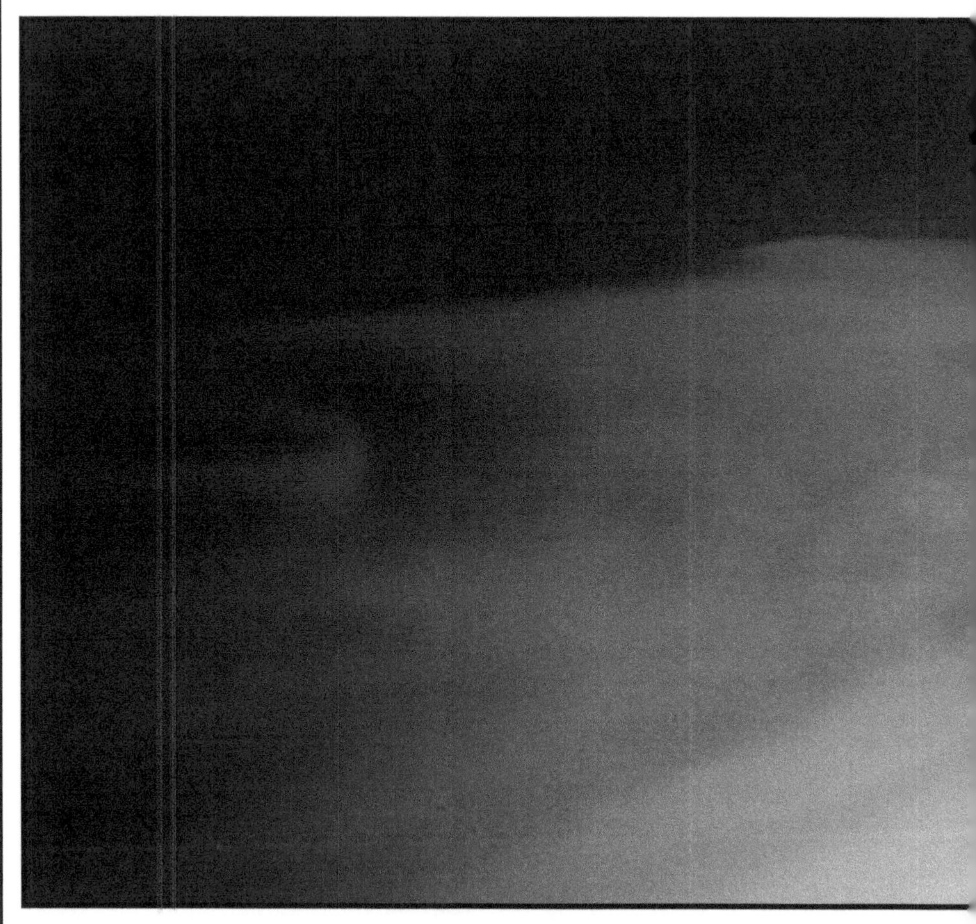

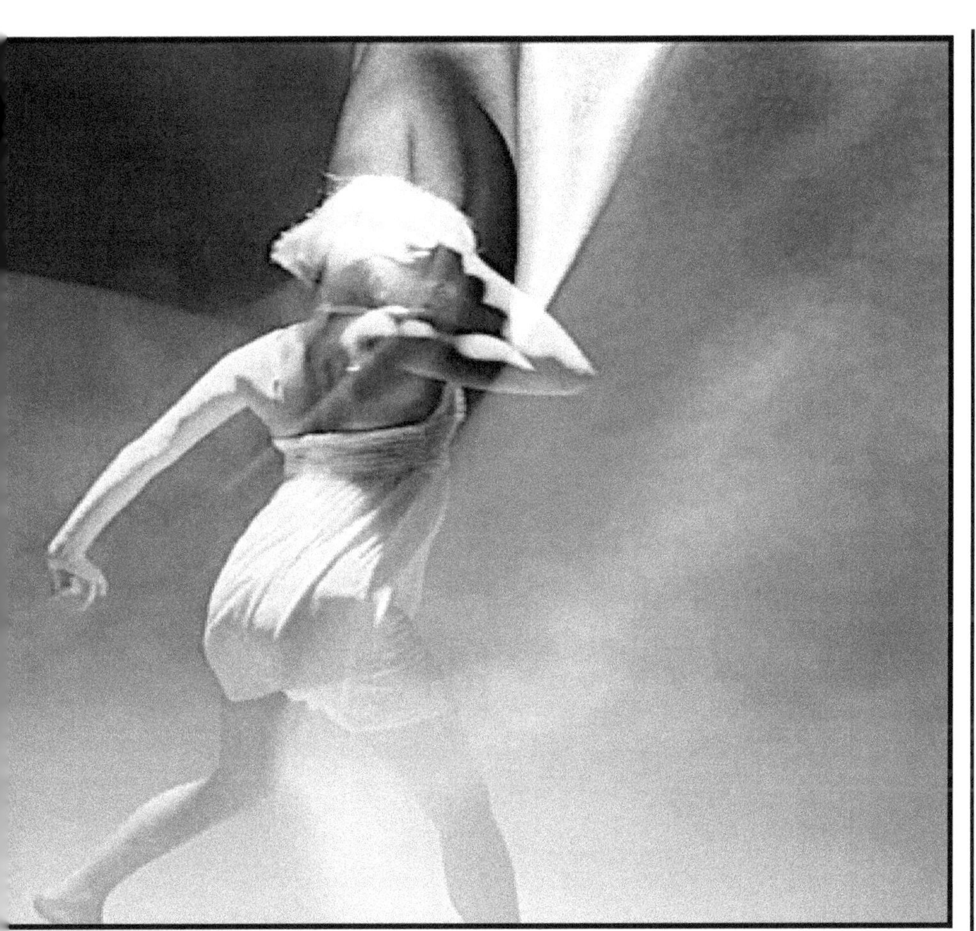

To my daughters, as two lost souls on the sinking Titanic, third party witnesses to the love saga and imminent death of Jack Dawson and Rose DeWitt Bukater

Erica Hoffmeister

We imagine ourselves as one of two things:

Jack
or
Rose

First Class
or
Steerage

Captive
or
Savior

Iceberg
or
Ship

Survivor
or
Deceased

In love
or
about to be

Imagine yourself for a moment, instead, as anything in between:

As anything is possible.

As the frigid water of the Atlantic streaming across black steel as a ship's hull slices through your being.

As cardboard cutout placement for late-90s CGI technology which will fill your body parts in with computer graphics as you stand silently in front of a green screen.

As fly on the wall. A flea on a rat.

As costume designer, as seamstress, as a Kate-shaped mannequin.

As the skin-drenched hand placed on the chest of a loved one while violent waters surge beneath.

As a fork stuck into a slab of marbled meat in the First Class Dining Saloon on D Deck.

As the slab of meat.

As yourself, wandering the decks filled with passengers, unknowing. Or, better, shattering
the fourth wall. Either way, you are wearing a petticoat. Either way, someone, somewhere, is falling in love.

Notice how normal this all feels, despite imminence, despite doom: the sky is clear and someone
has smuggled lodestone in their muslin pocket. Its vibrations hum over iron in a leitmotif
you can't quite place.

A streak of red hair, a momentary dance
with the smell of charcoal sticks and
clean, diamond-cut ice chunks,
clanking crystal cheers drifting the image
down-deck

Notice how no one else notices

A tossed table, broken porcelain shards in baby-soft palms
a child lost, a child saved
by the same hands, the same lie
captive in flesh-molds of whale bone rib cages
until fire-edged silk and
smudged window-lust
draw you into smug clichés of star-crossed
lovers and superlunary, pit-in-the-belly
yearning

defining naïve romantic expectations

when a frenzied flare
shot into a placid sky
conflates possibility of
fireworks or comet tails or panic
—the heart beats the same tempo

an entire spectacle of

love

a ship built around

a massive
man-made vessel
infallible
you know it's

fate

a coping mechanism

a naturally occurring obstacle
creating a wreckage on the bottom of the sea.

Imagine yourself as two of two things:

Ship
and
Sea

Plot
and
Foil

Iron
and
Ice

Vessel
and
Trench

Discoverer
and
Excavated

Seeking a Caretaker

Steph Butchko

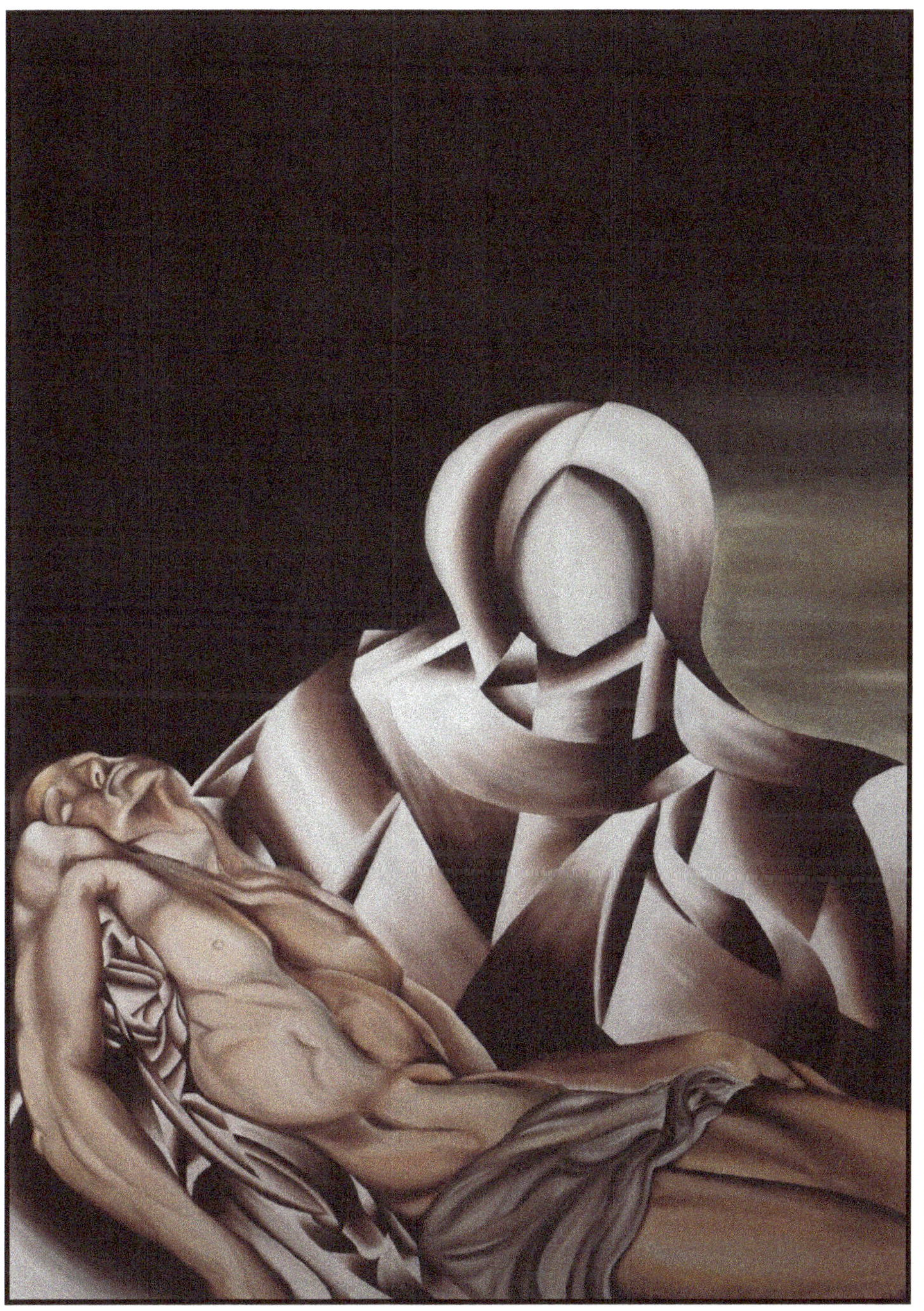

Pity, Mercy, Compassion

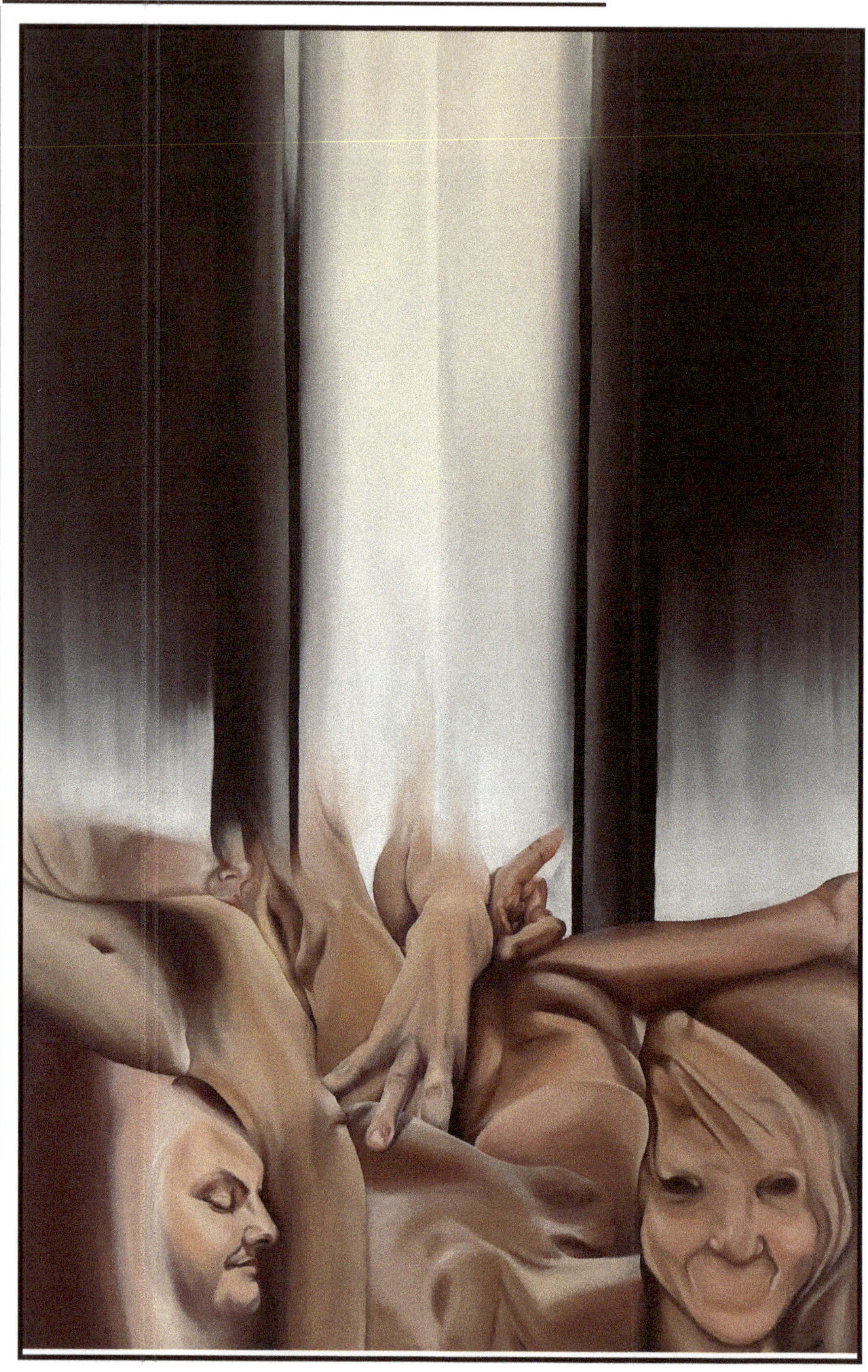

As Above

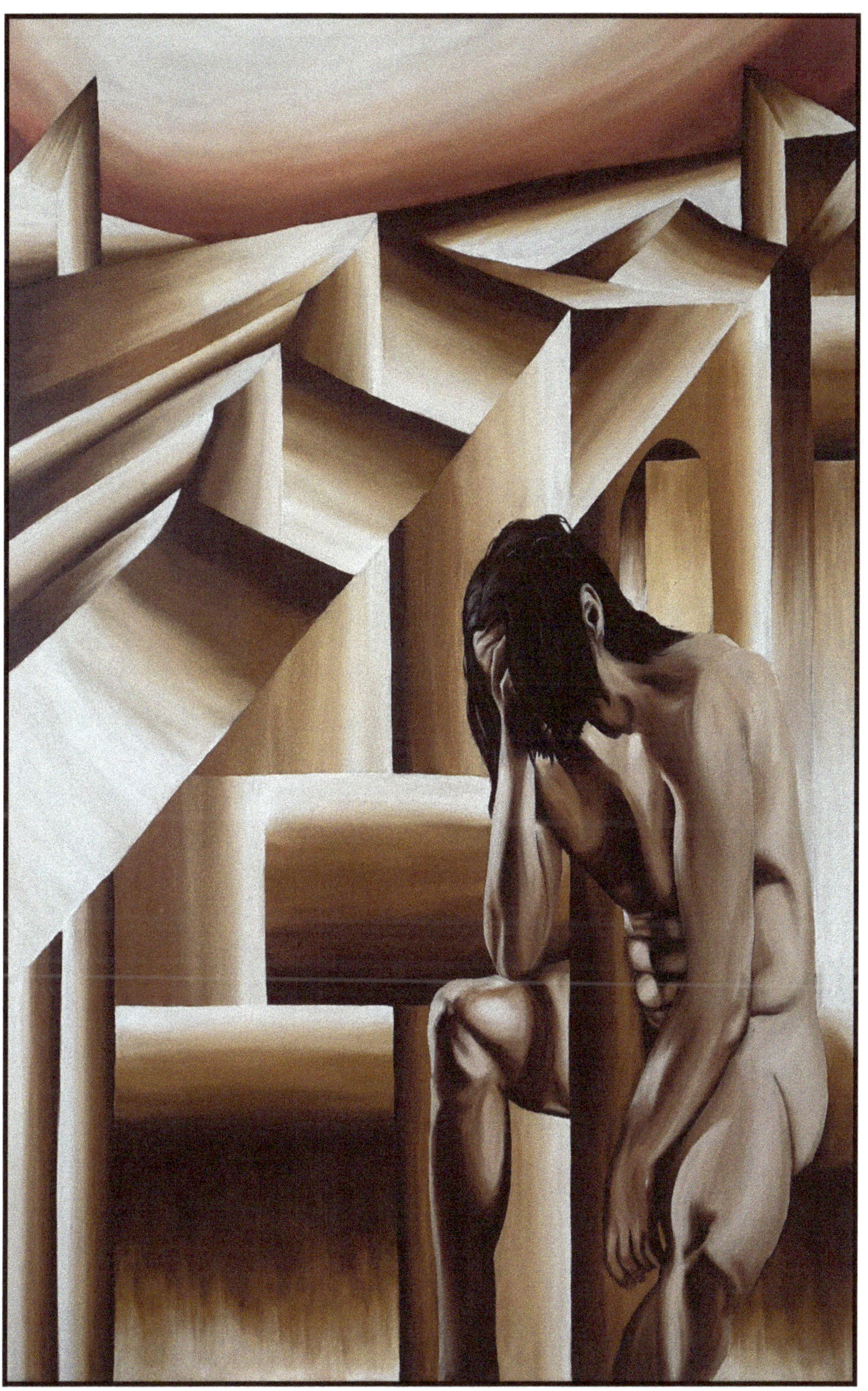

Waiting On The Woman To Give This Moment Purpose

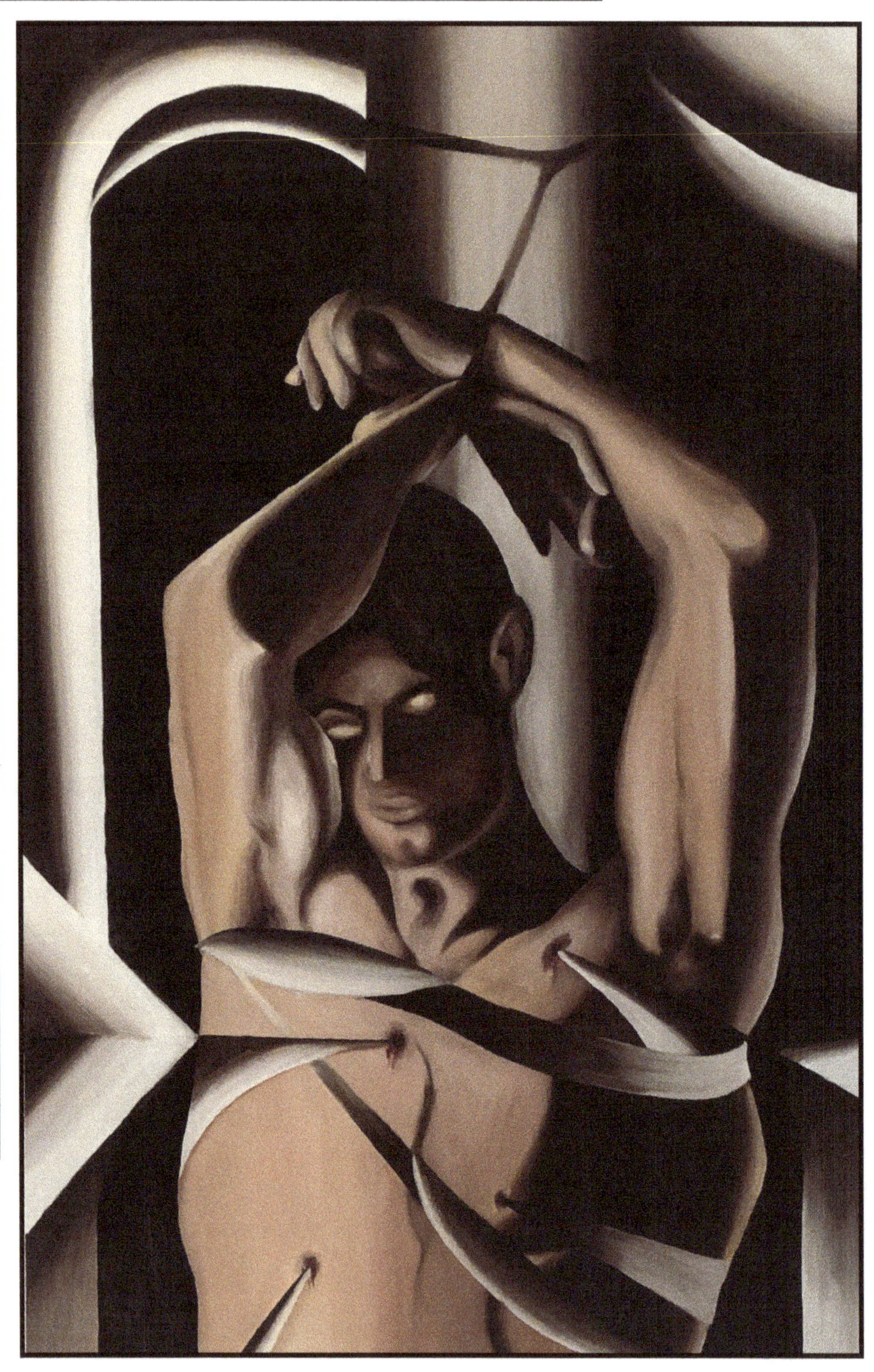

St. Sebastian

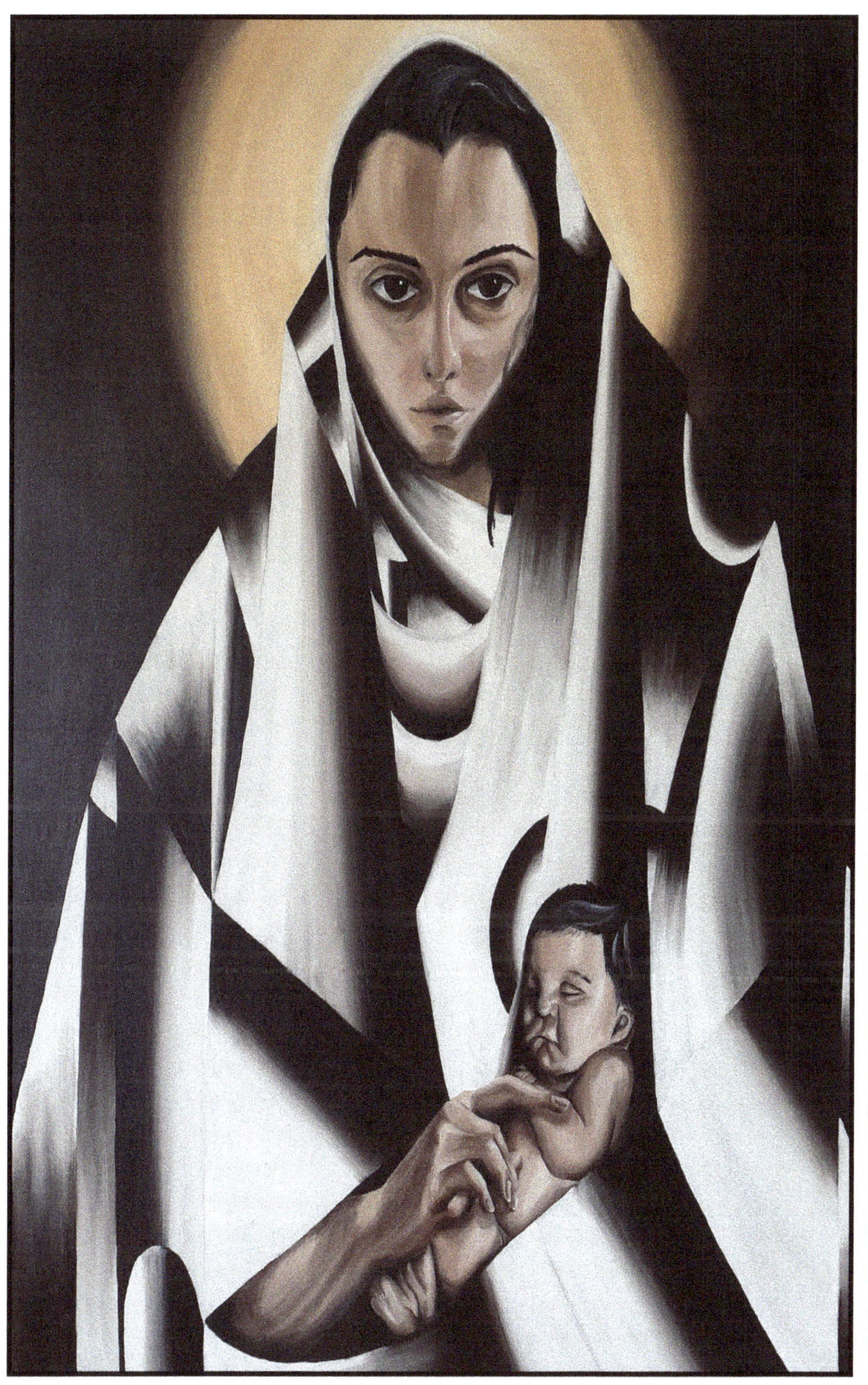

Madonna Of Humility

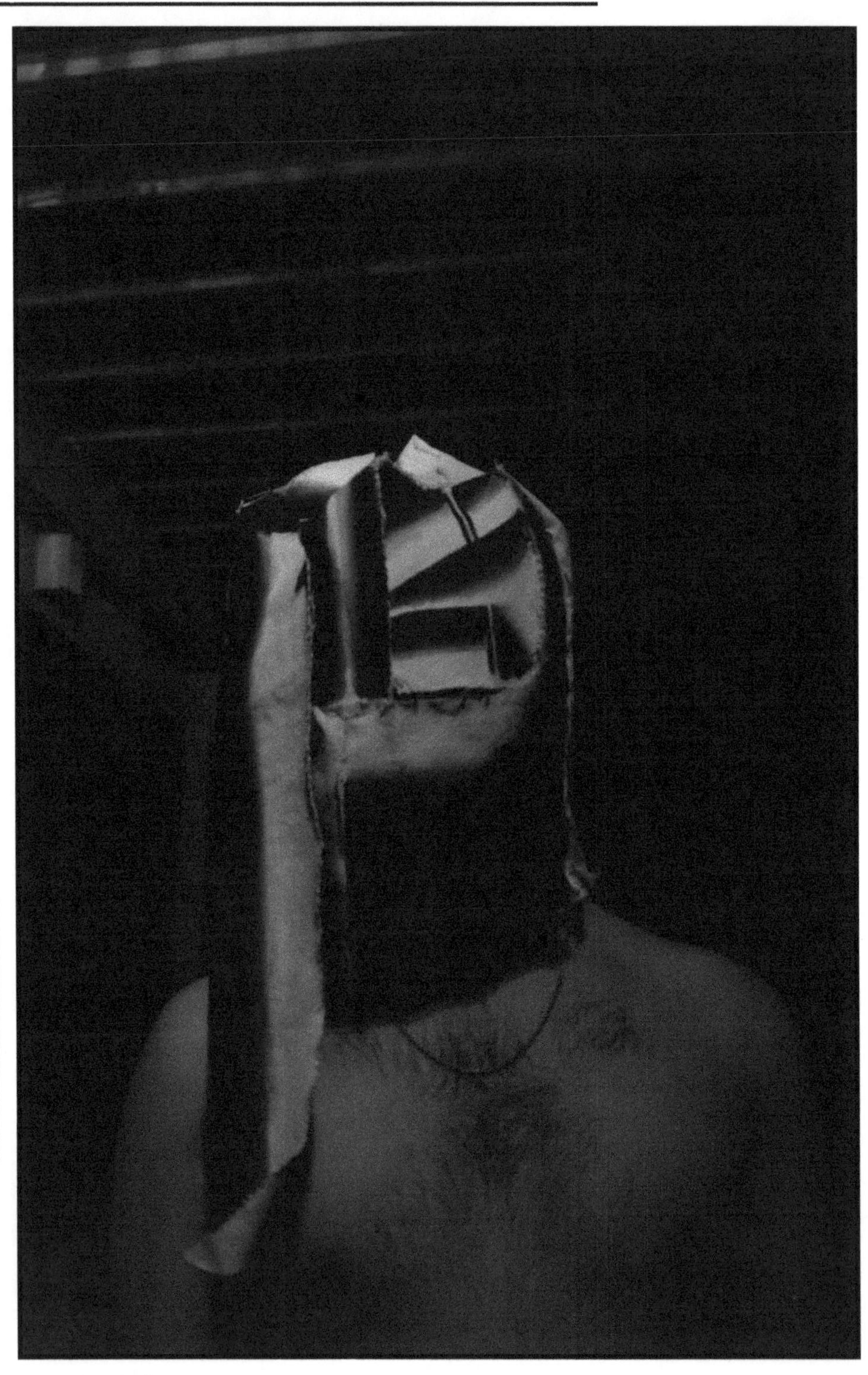

Masked

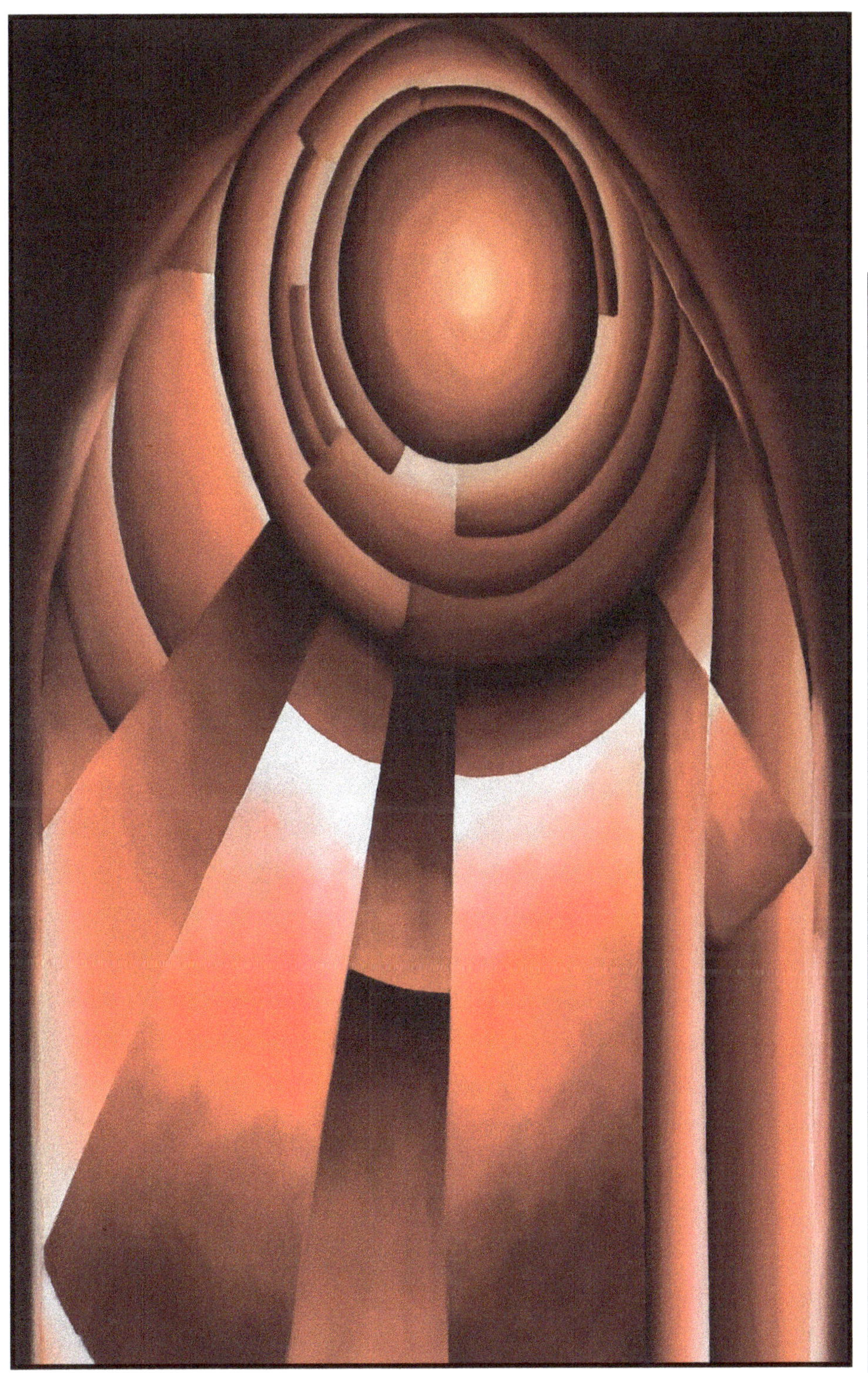

Sun

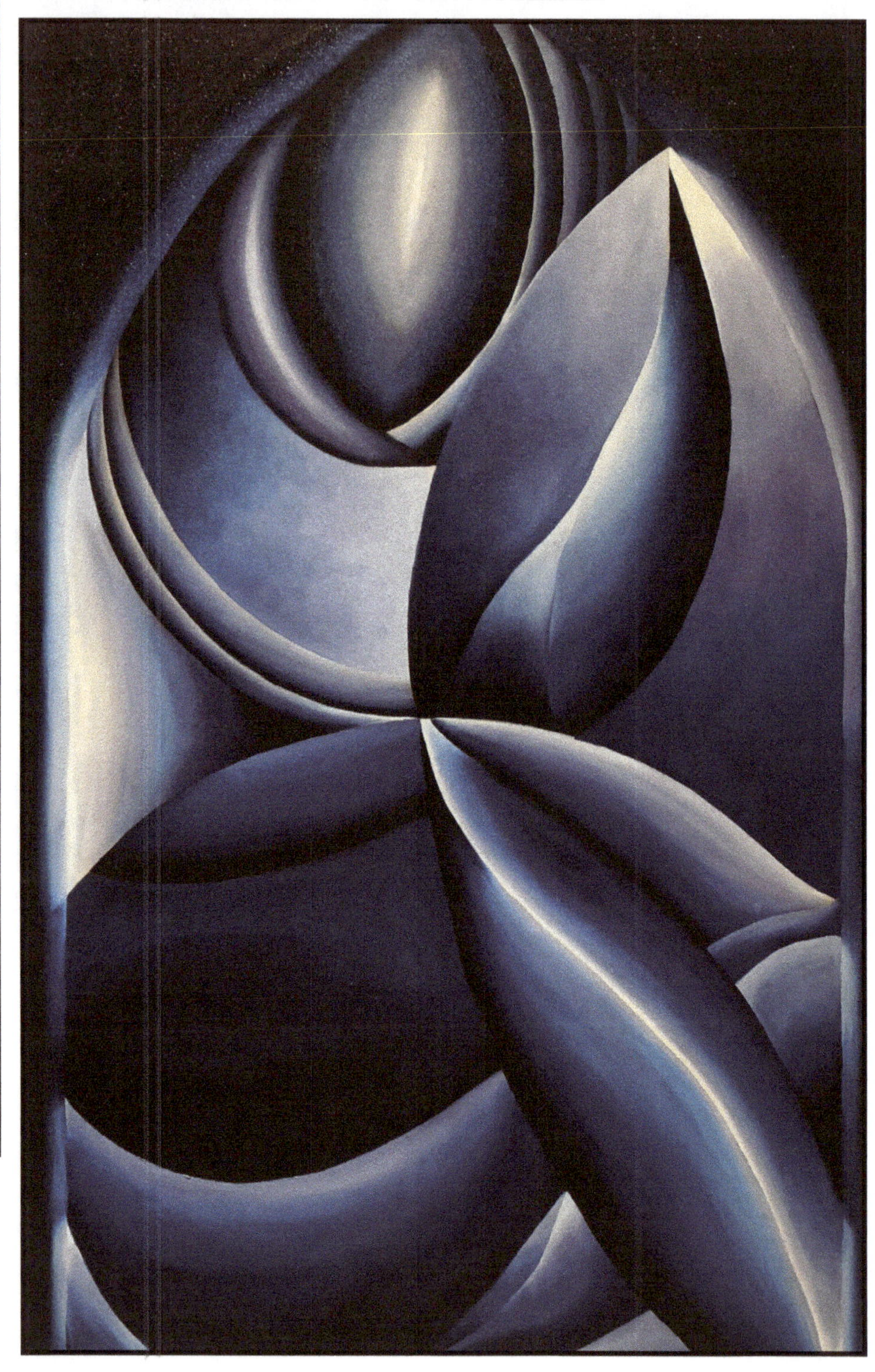

Moon

operating costs

Will Pewitt

Hold out your fear,
      a fable built of ink.
Don't let your hearts splutter.
                  No, green your shadow.
Stone your limbs.
Be as time:
      in every moving
         an asking.

But what futures ride in this request?
      So many sands in one,
none in another.
                  Where flew all the balance?
A composition of cries,
      breaths as vast as only   panic.
Purr a promise,
a sly suggestion.
But not   in letters,
where words steal all meaning.

So, ask:
Do you have touch
                where you come from?
Know you the
      proper way to scream?
How has my hand grown so small?
Can I share with you this flood,
        as soft as desperate?

You must excuse my manner, say.
It's been so long since I've tasted questions.

The Itch

J.B. Fredkin

The present dies
inside our bodies.

He came to visit
me in my dream,

our dog, long passed.
Us, long passed. He

darted into woods
I did not know.

I sprinted in pursuit,
followed him home,

just knowing it was
home and he was

alive and there
you were. There

are moments so
profound only

a body could know
they ever happened.

Here: it all exists,
billows then burns

up in black chambers
beyond the mountain

that pumps existence.
Please, wake up.

Beach Picnic

Charles Miller

I watched as you pulled on your jet black chelsea boots

and the bottom of your foot looked at me anew,

cracked, newly parched in spite of the rain outside.

Tears in a great new age.

We had dreams of dark wood cabinets once

long driveways leading to porches.

Now the second oldest of us leaves,

some old sentiment of wisdom and simplicity

ranging in desert tones and roan sweetnesses of the eyes.

Stifled kisses turn end over end with promises.

I have not seen you since,

we were unaware and unknown, sickly with our own meanings.

Trauma was our center.

Feeling word's edges with empty, sandy fingers,

nothing was again clean.

Desert Triptych

Paula Camacho

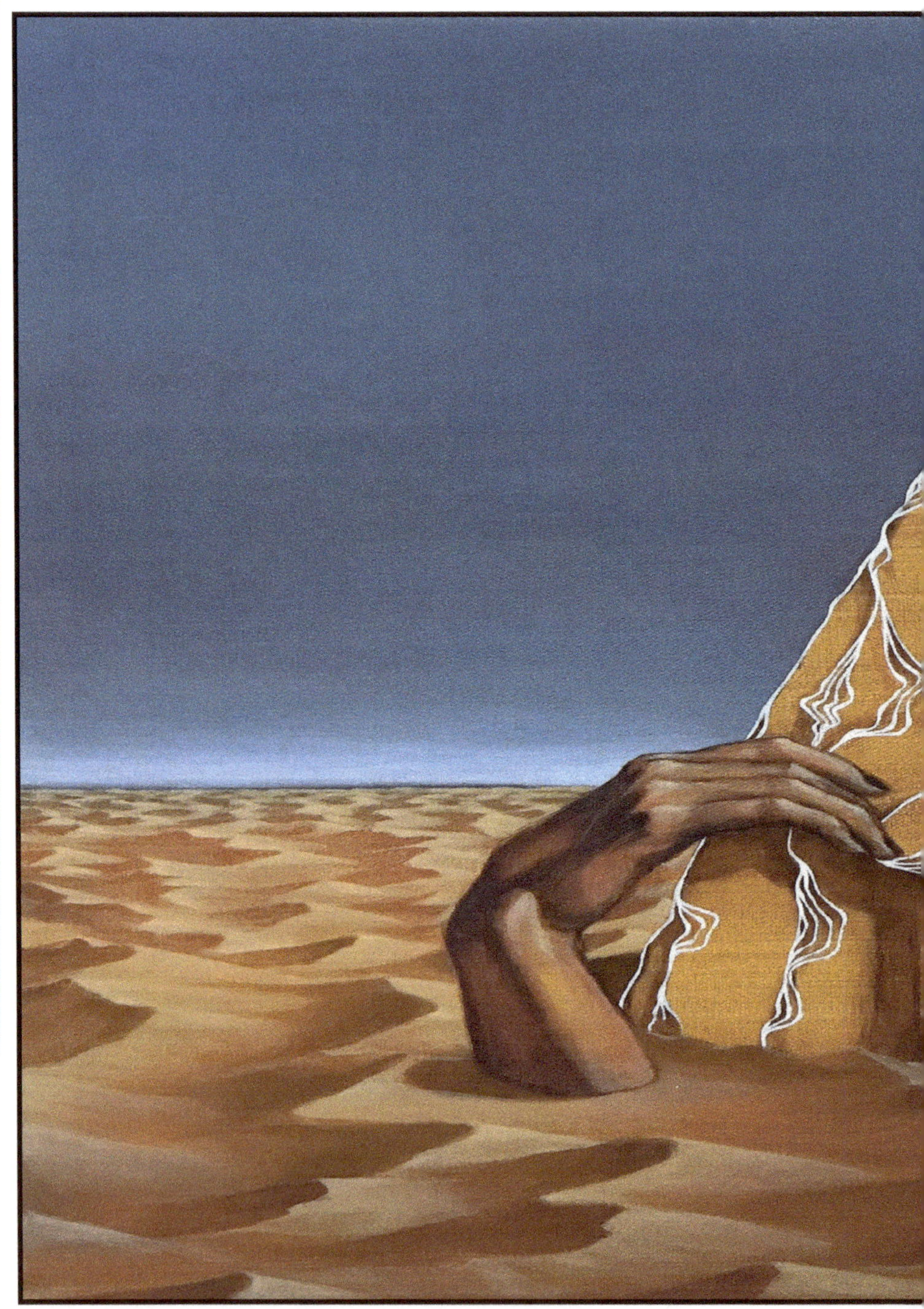

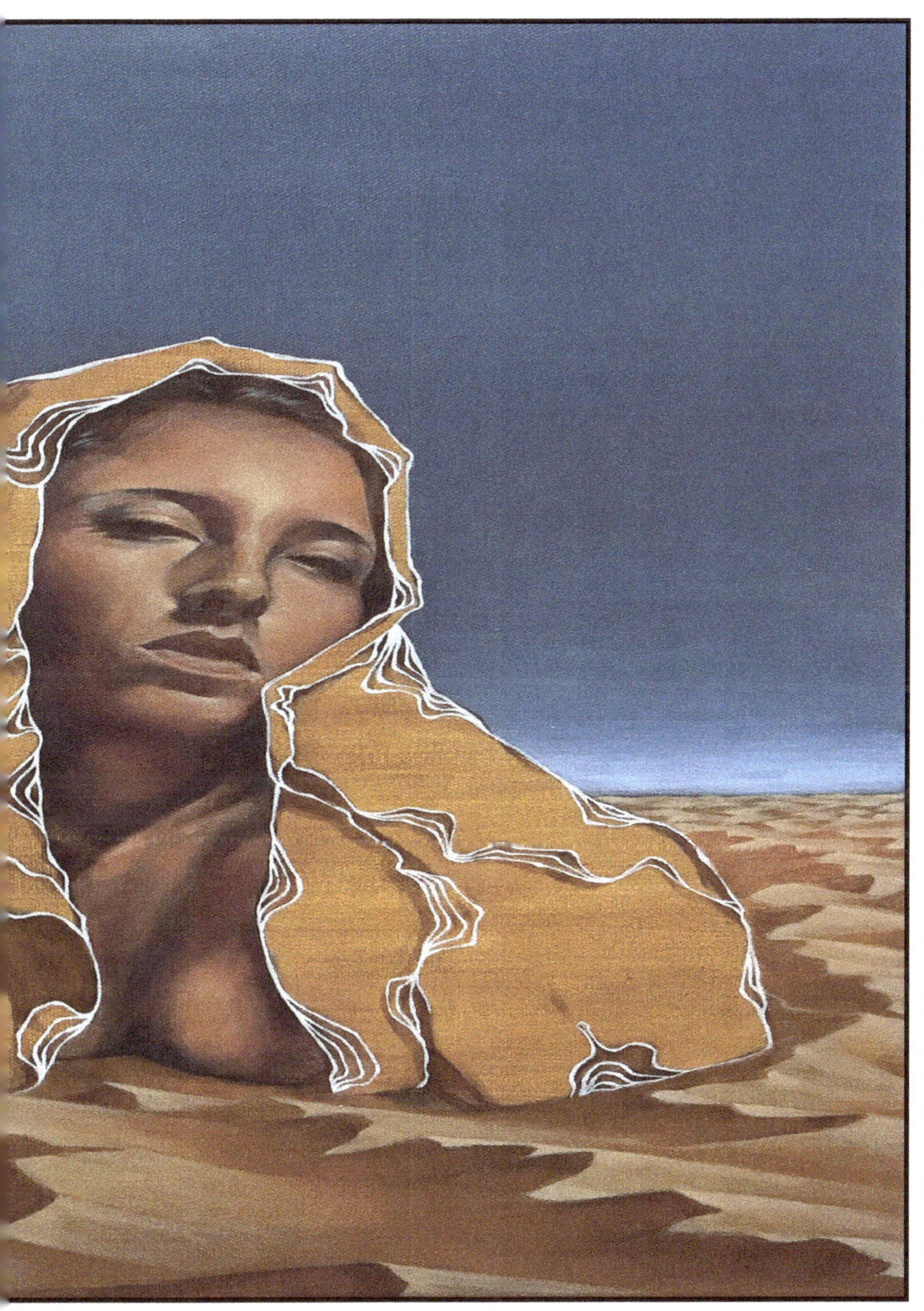

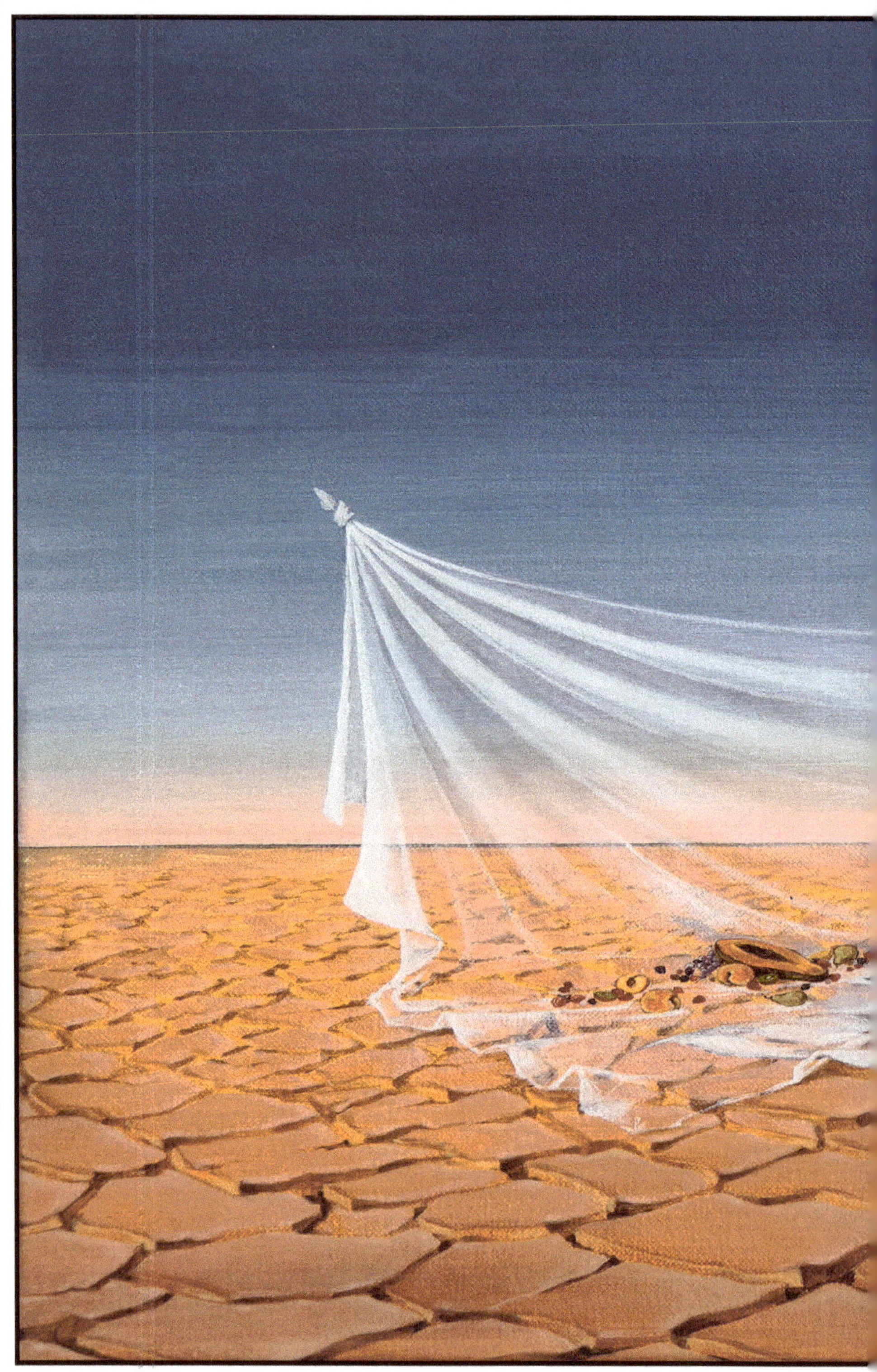

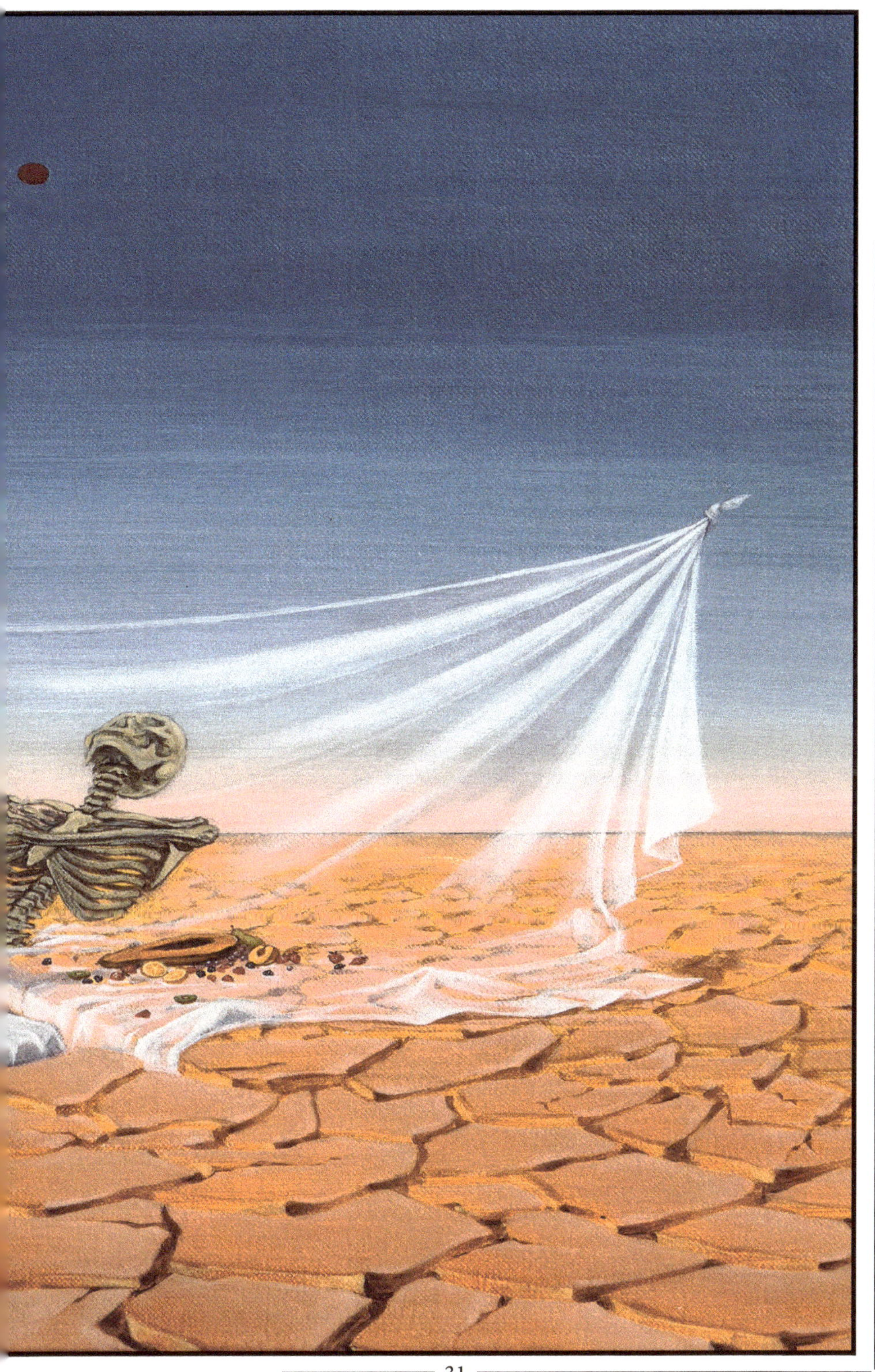

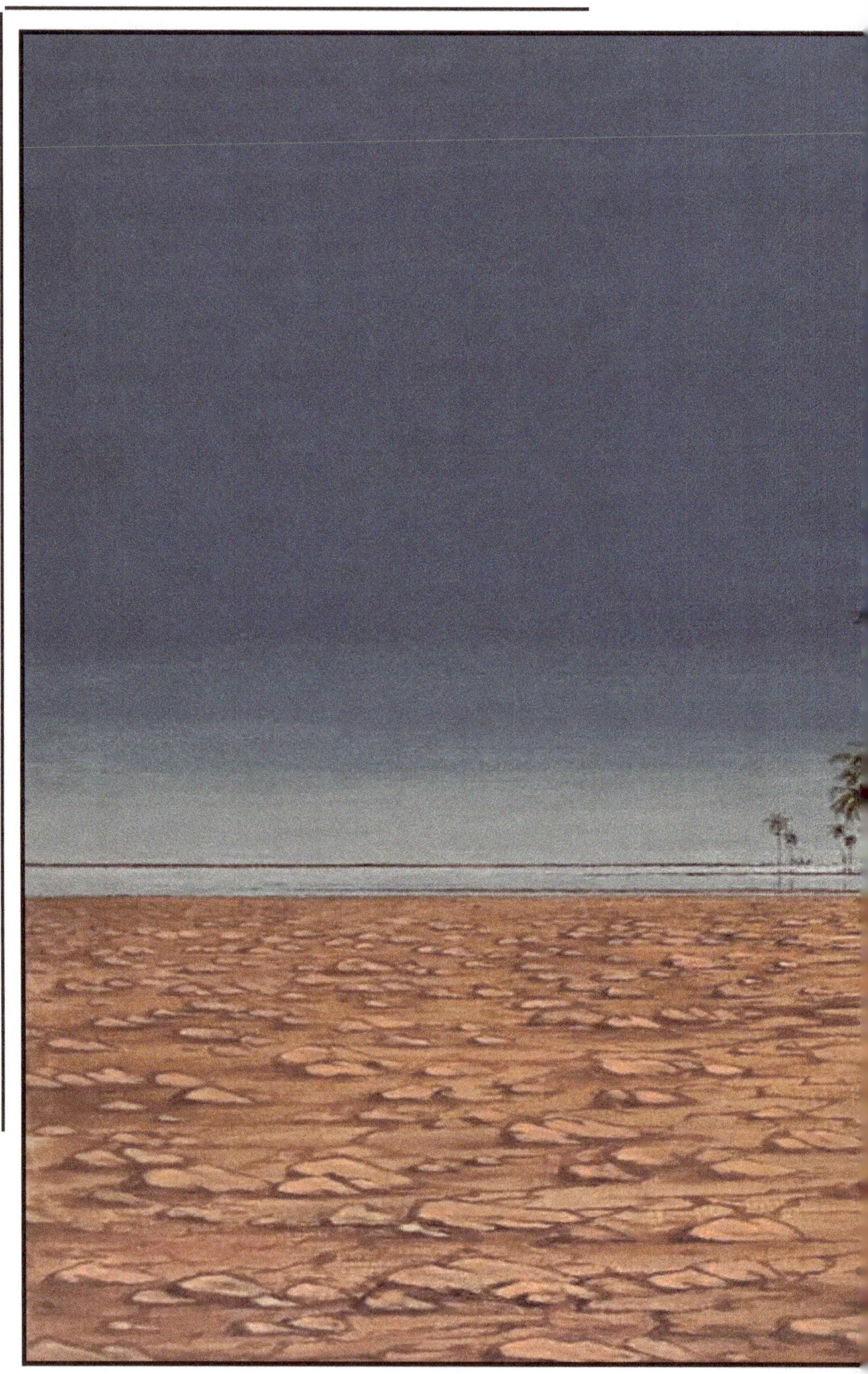

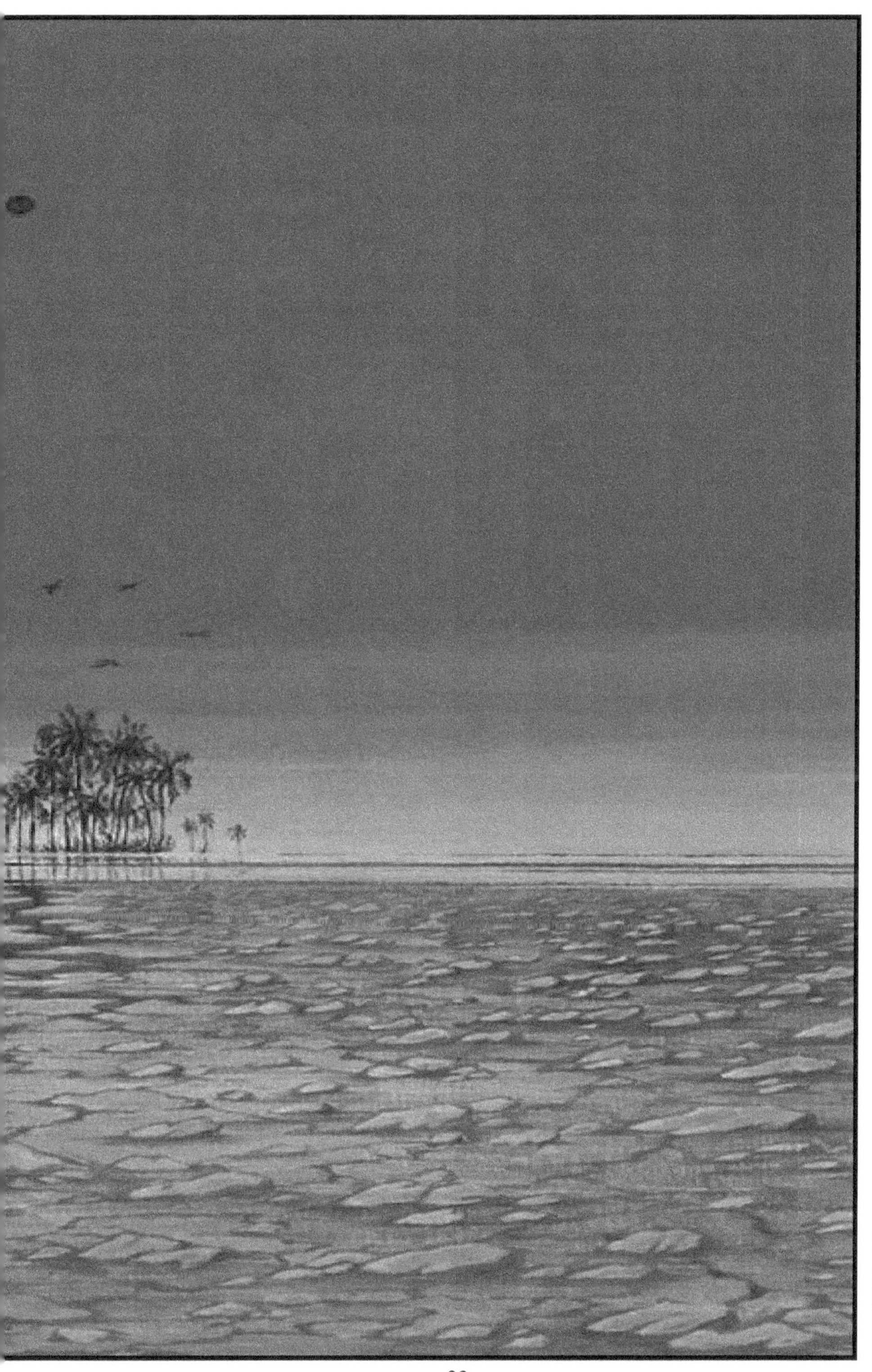

I Am the Earth

Josalyn Switzer

because I formed the same way.
A solar nebula compressed itself,
heat growing in a night-womb.

After all the violent contractions,
our solar system was born.
Shining star sliced from a torso after

the Sun choked on heavenly bodies.
Cells were thrown together, particles flying
through space, colliding over and over to make

planetesimals. I am made of syllables, words
like burning radiation, "I want you to look svelte,"
or like oxygen, "I'll love you forever."

Words became sentences, then moments,
then memories, all colliding and combining
to make the spinning planet of my thoughts.

Earth kept growing, pulled more experiences
toward it, built itself up layer by layer. A world
dreaming of the future and the voice it finally built.

Time was the first ingredient.
Patience until the Earth began to
nurture its ideas into passions.

A hot lava under its skin, it changed
its own surface, perspective, resilience.
I push tectonic plates, build my own

mountains out of memoirs. The nebula
didn't know what it was in for.
It threw out specks of life and got

me. A fire filled planet being
changed by each moment, but staying
true to my chosen orbit.

paperman

Yeonjae (Jeannie) Eom

it starts with a punch
to the gut
hacking cough spitting
curse and gasp
slipping between barbed tongues
and the cracks of skin smoke-dry

it feels like a blow
shut doors–sometimes metal bars
batons to abdomen
bowing where eye meets earth–
soiled with paw prints of man–
and breaths count numbers on one hand

eyes unclosed
half sea water half liquor
so crystal clear the reflections of irises
glitter pages written by cops and bastards
while the heartbeats on the monitor's lines
meet grim reapers and angels

between the collective memory
and the lives of vile truth
blank pages fill the gap
long enough that by the end
no man remembers each blow
and each breath

until it is written in
with thick black ink
no page of reservation
fingers tracing sharp edges
rounding
red cuts healing in black streaks

it ends with renewal
like springs–bodies recoil
but when broken bones mend
fissures plastered together
with pages of raw truth
baring the wings of history

the wind picks up under
and the paperman flies

Recent Work

Chris Rekrutiak

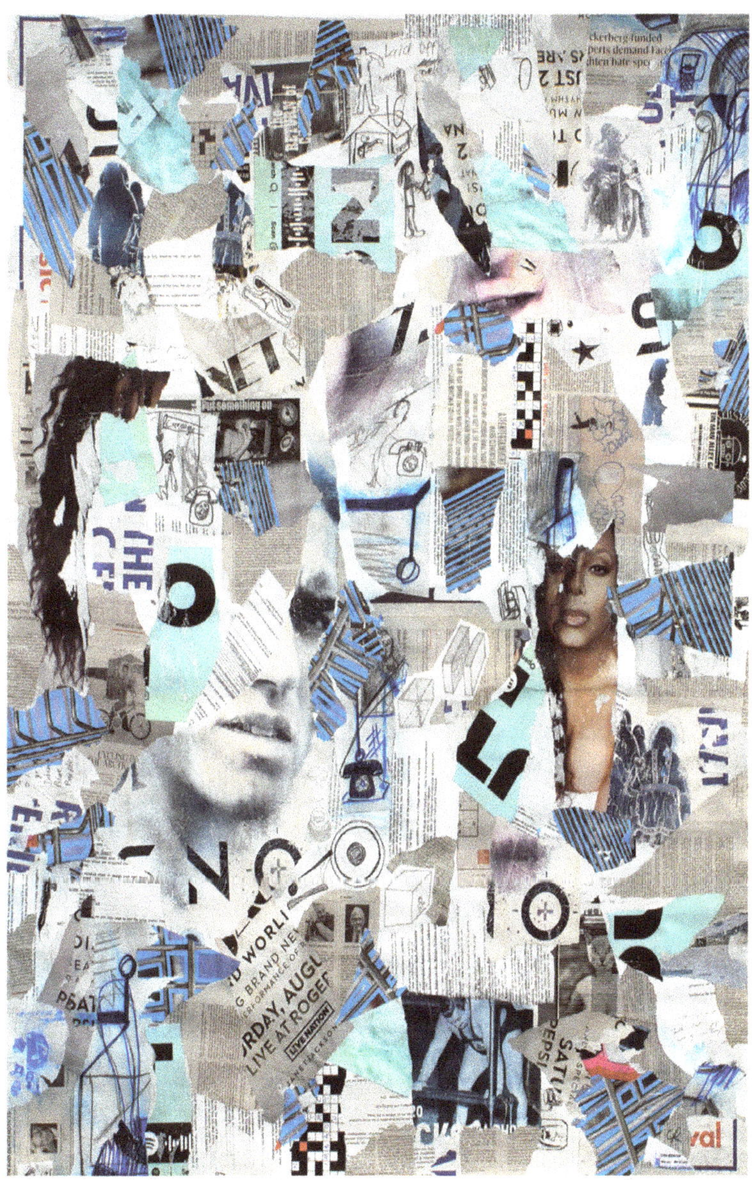

White Male Obituary
Chris Rekrutiak, 2020
Mixed Media on Paper
117cm x 94cm

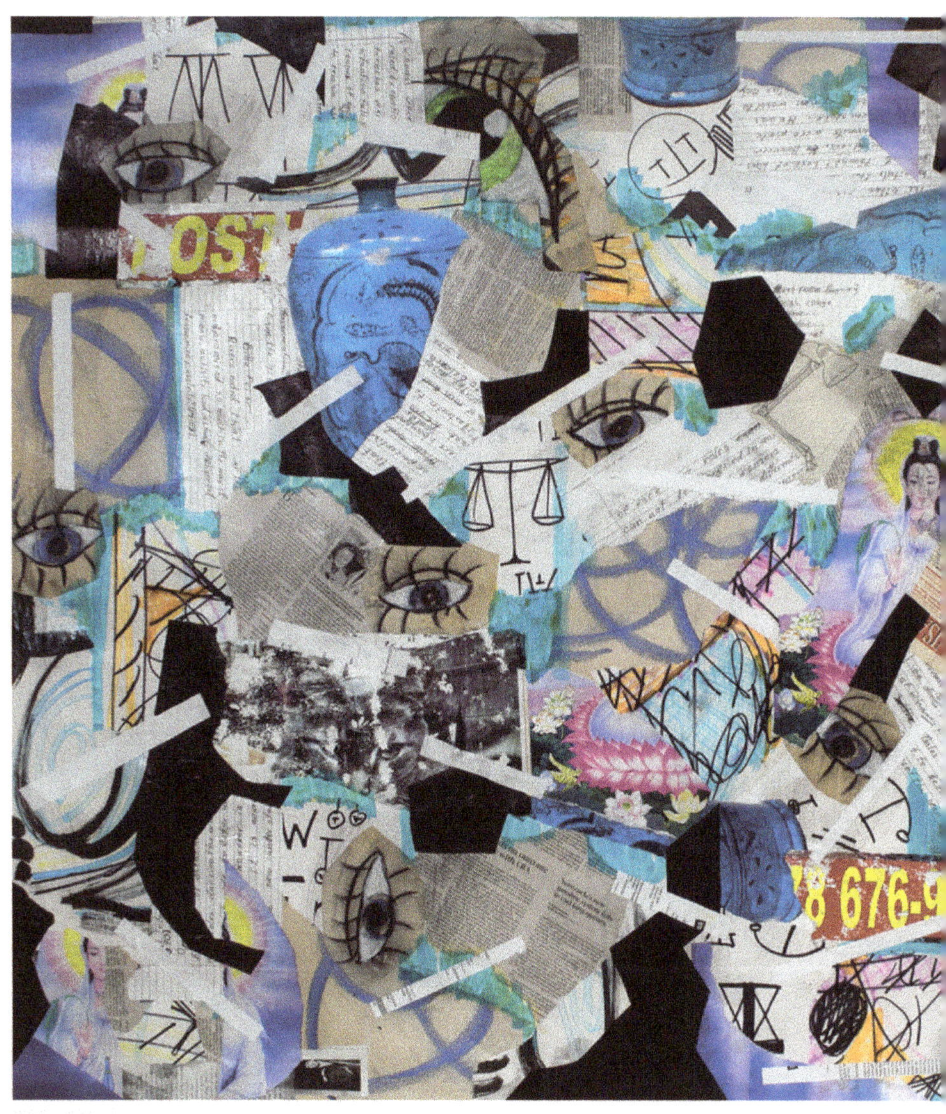

What to Lose
Chris Rekrutiak, 2020
Mixed Media on Paper
195cm x 105cm

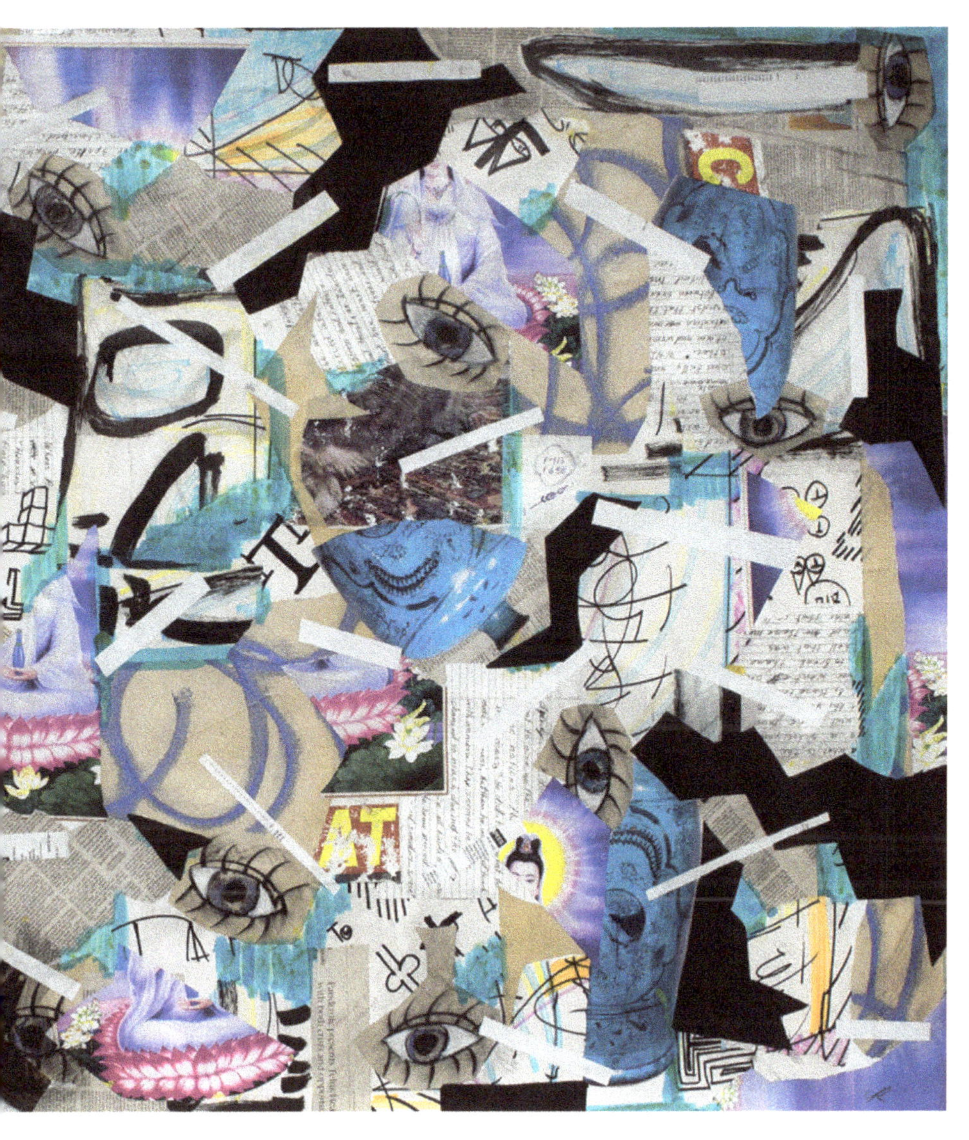

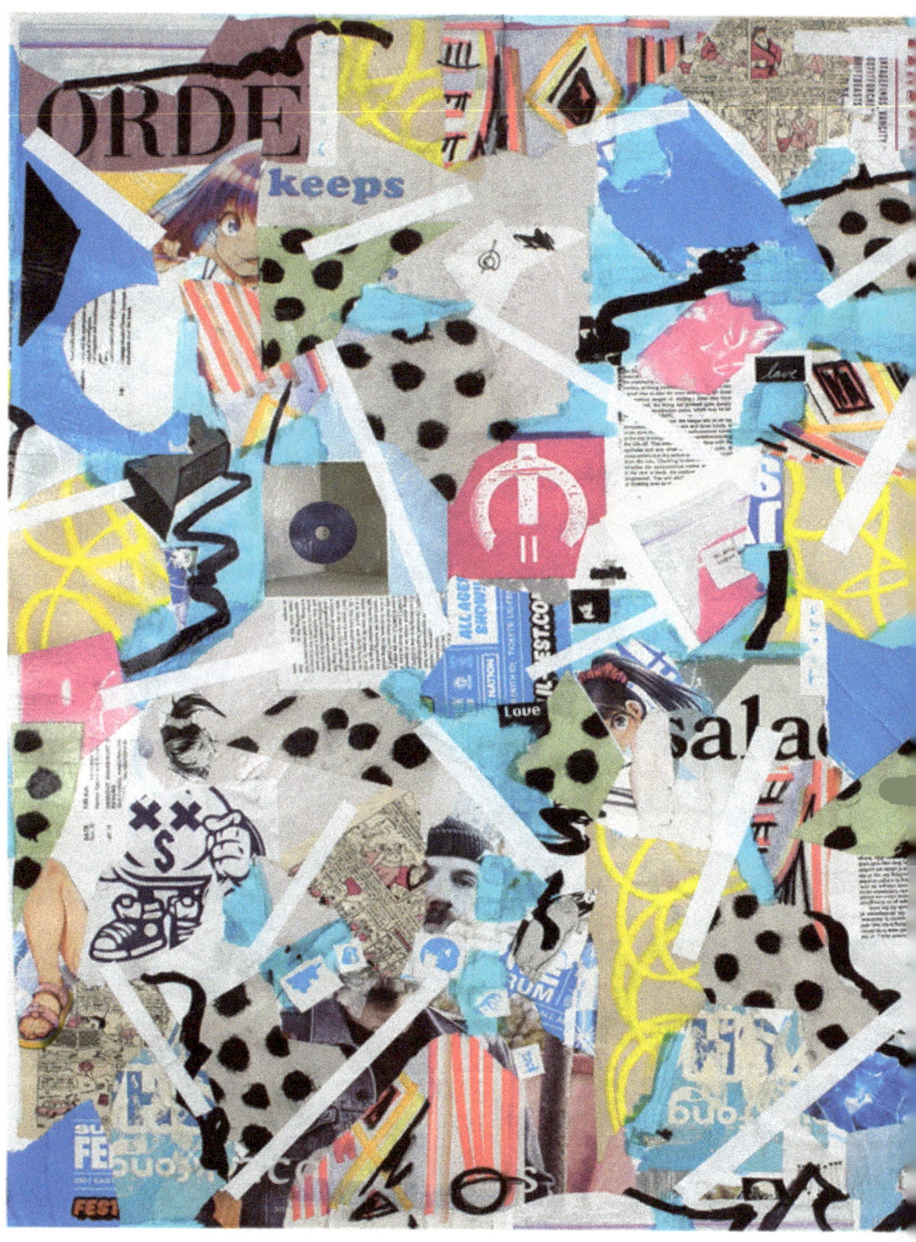

The Cost of Getting Nowhere

Chris Rekrutiak, 2020
Mixed Media on Paper
146cm x 105cm

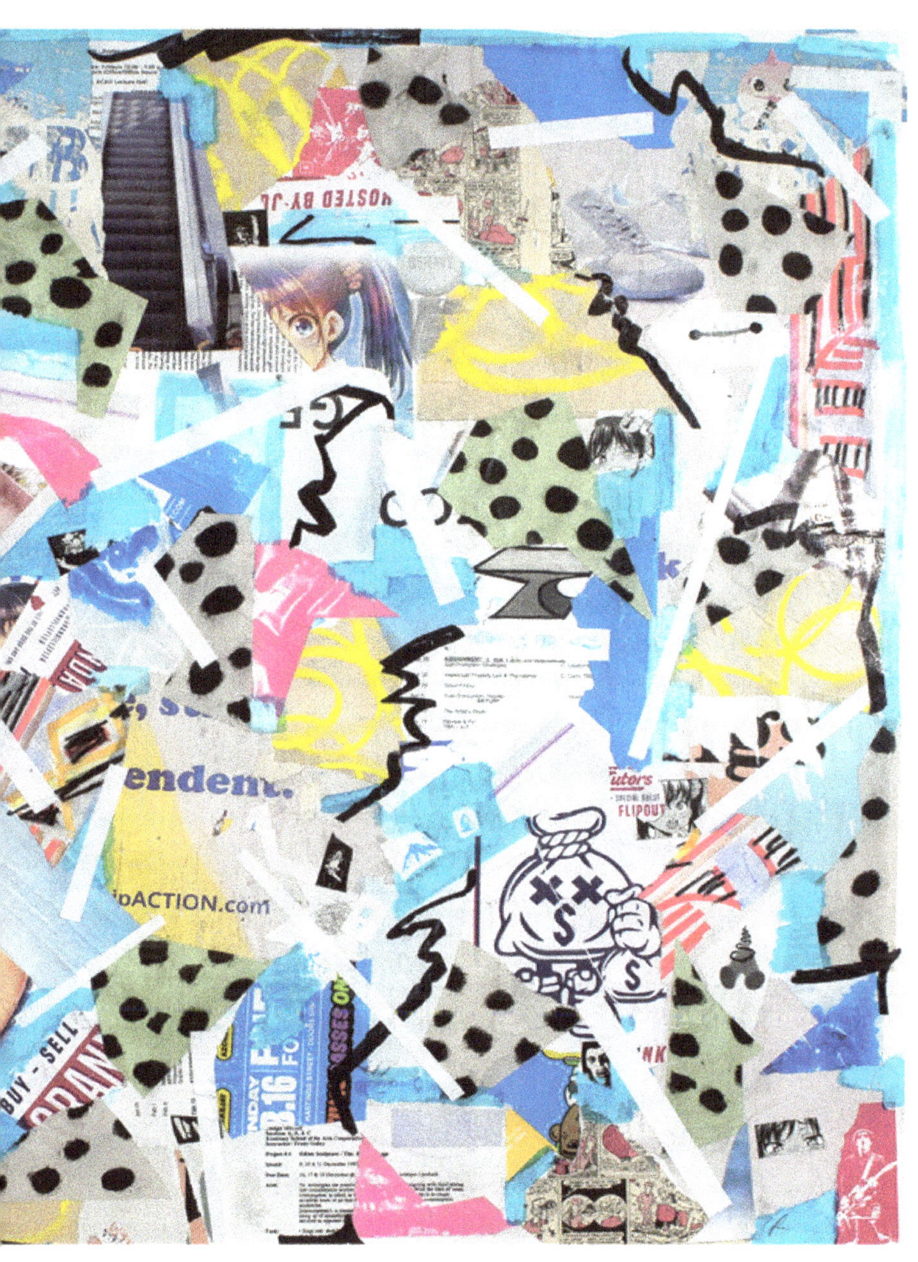

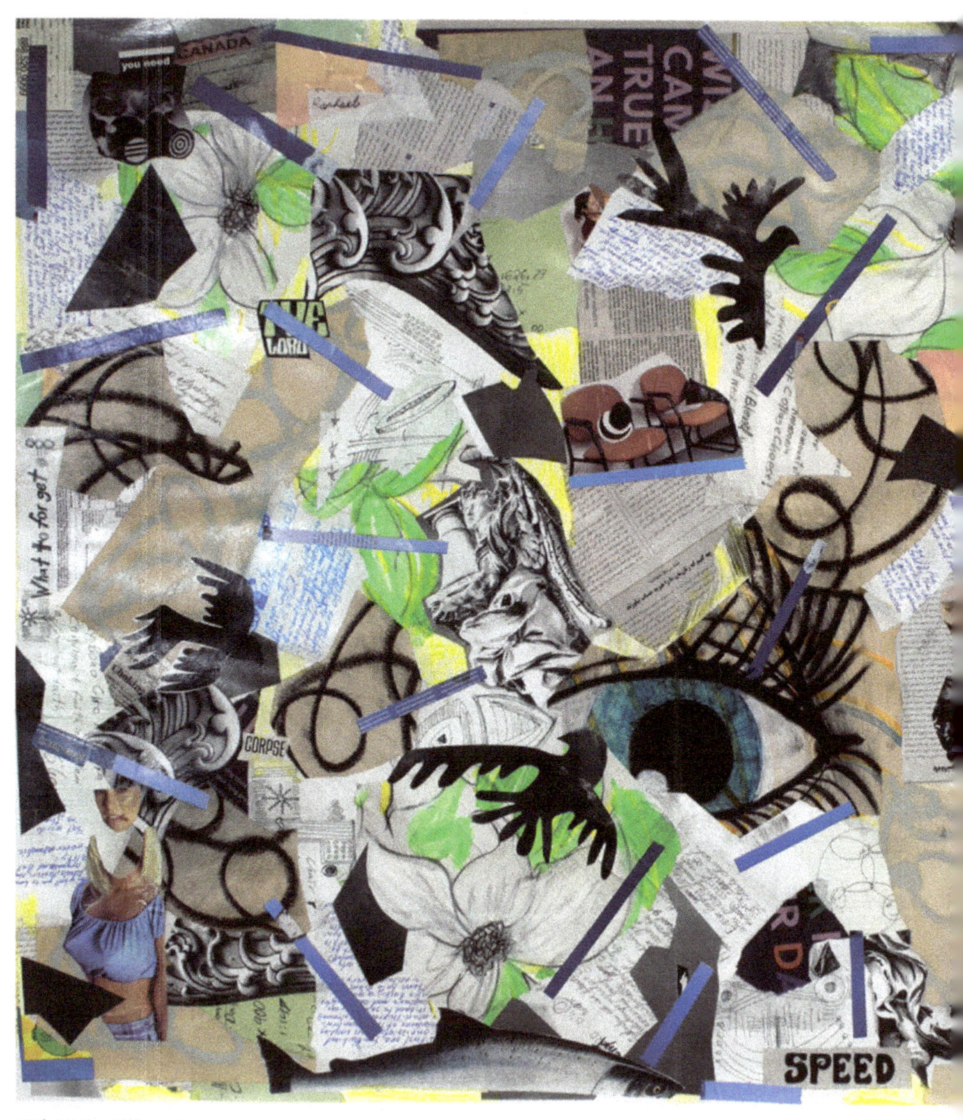

What to Forget

Chris Rekrutiak, 2020
Mixed Media on Paper
195cm x 105cm

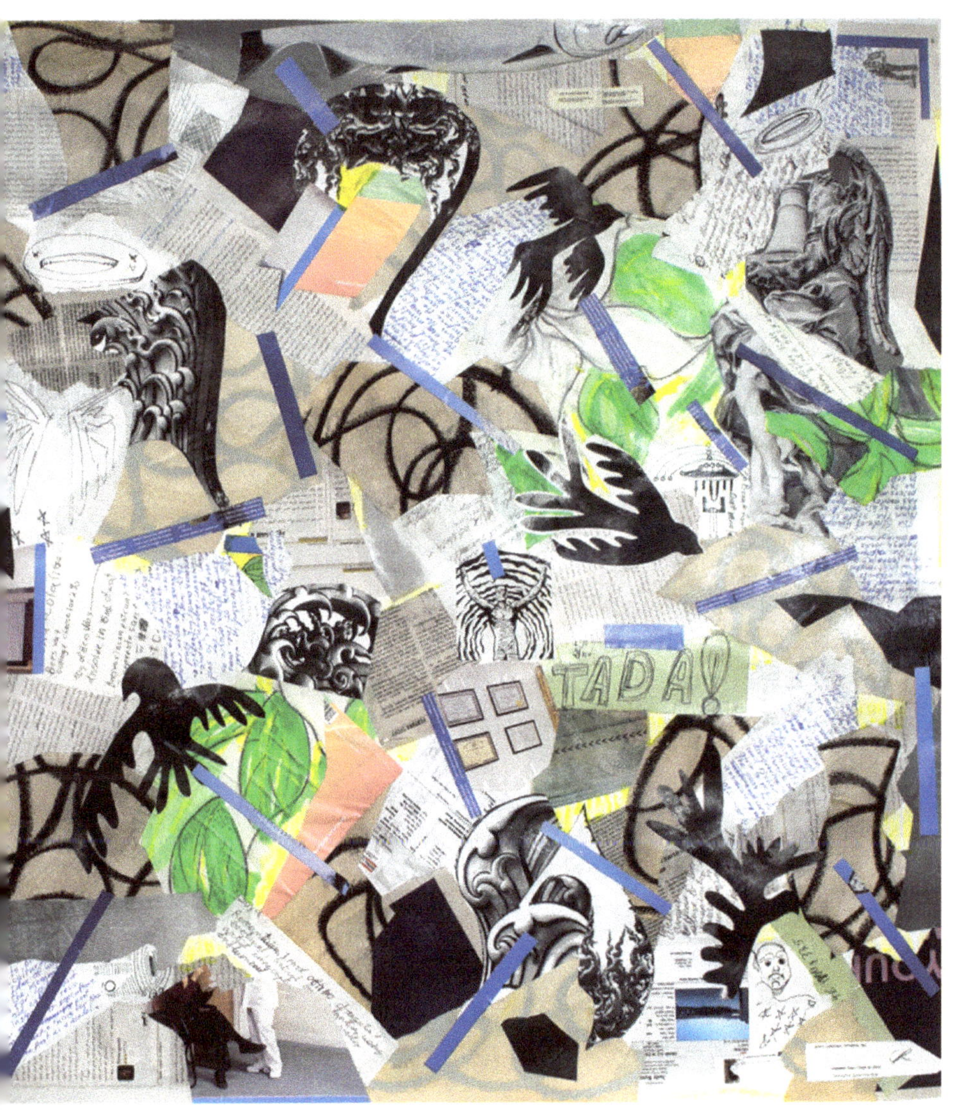

TADA!

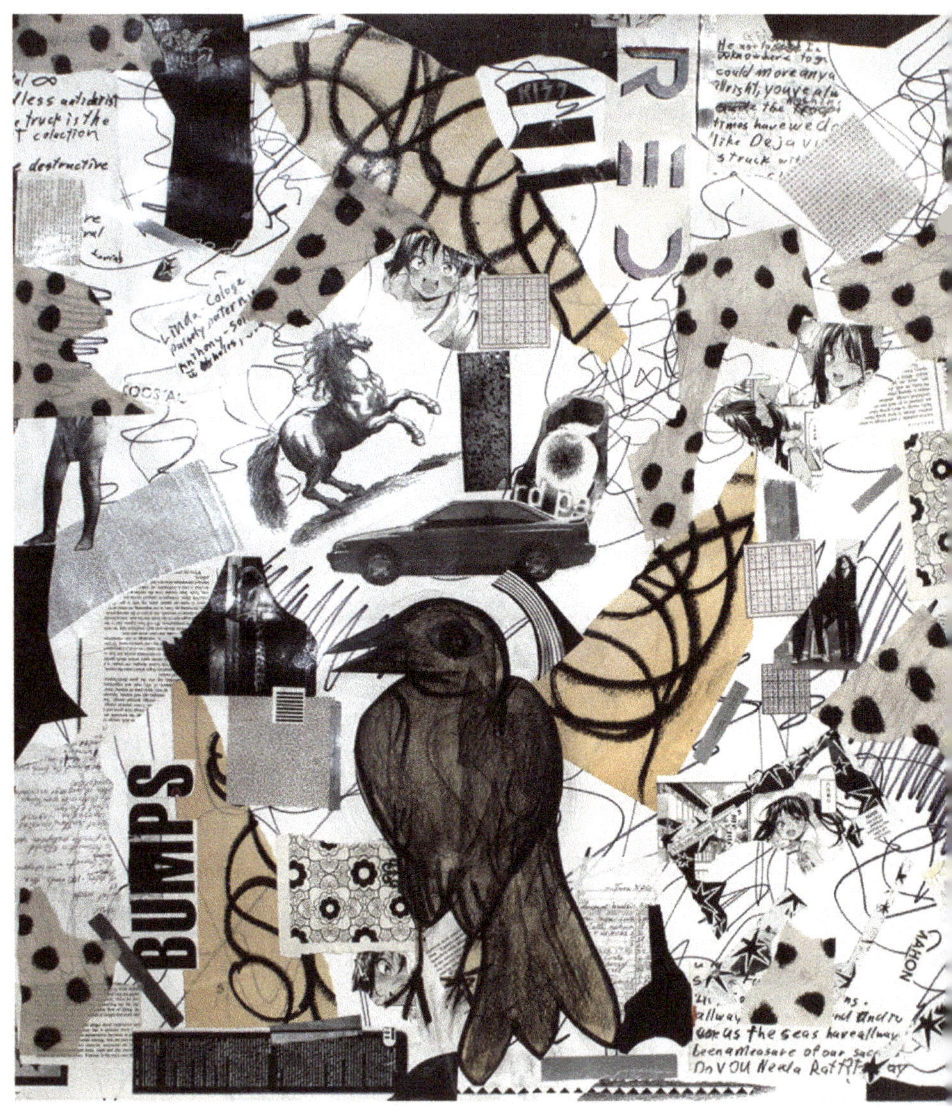

Ford Motors

Chris Rekrutiak, 2020
Mixed Media on Paper
195cm x 105cm

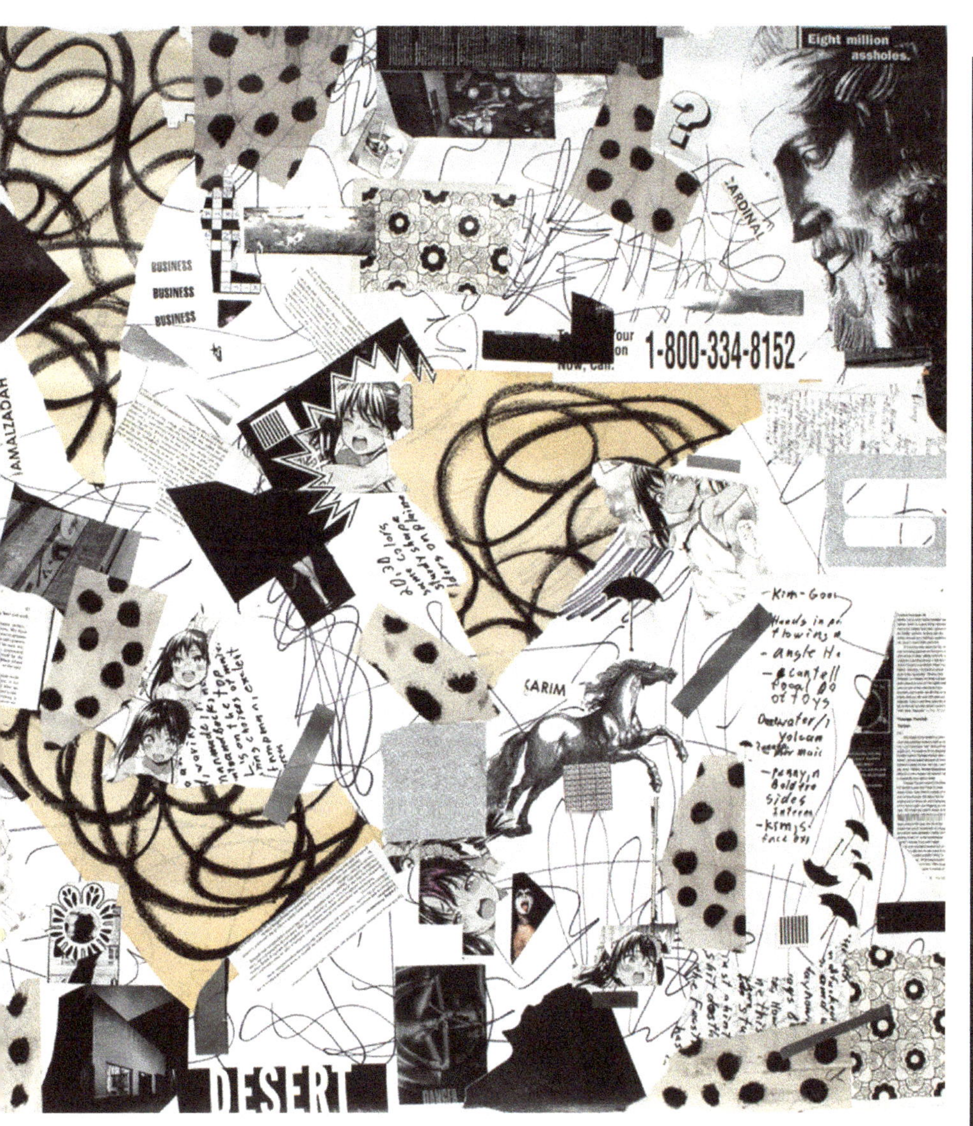

Eight million assholes.
BUSINESS
BUSINESS
BUSINESS
CARDINAL
1-800-334-8152
DESERT

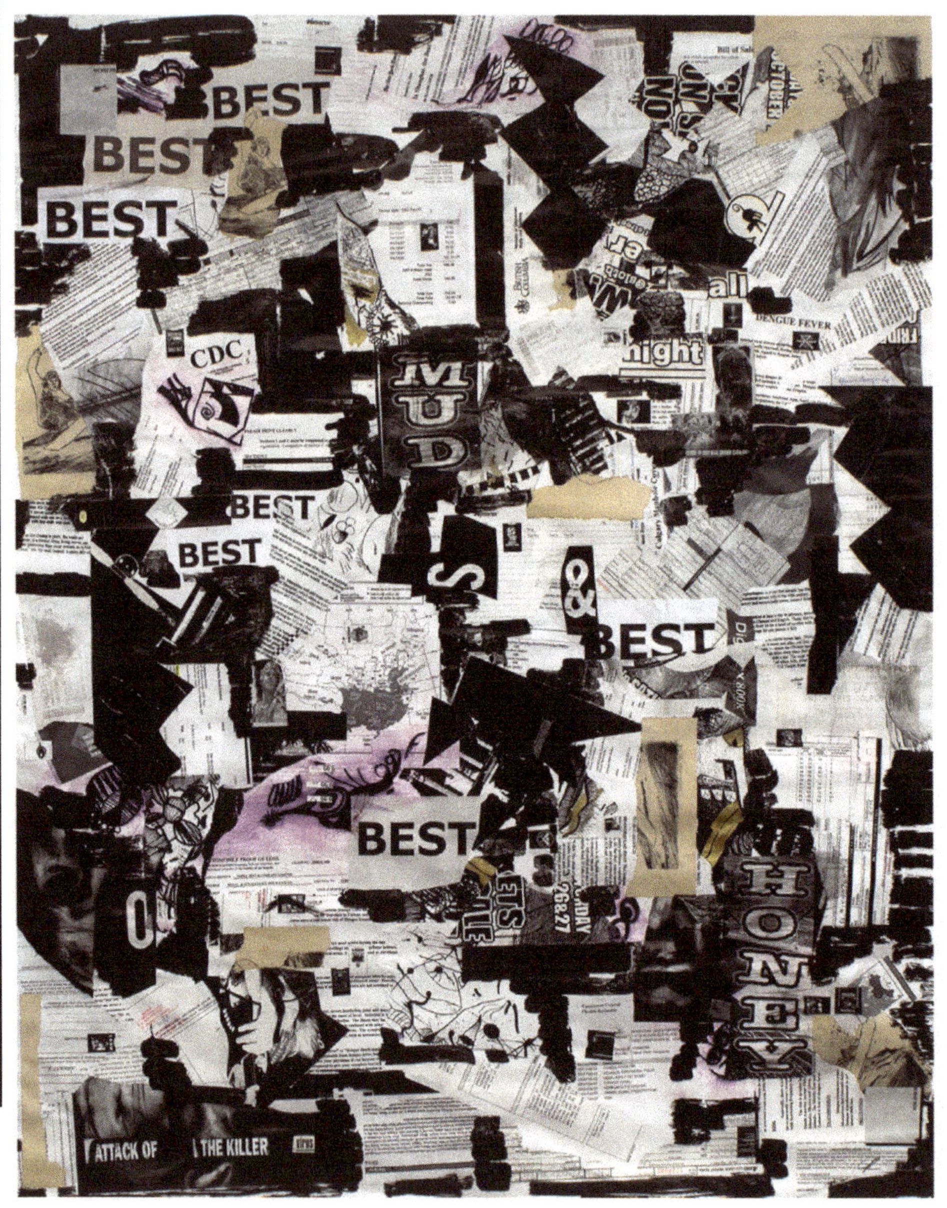

Teenager
Chris Rekrutiak, 2020
Mixed Media on Paper
117cm x 94cm

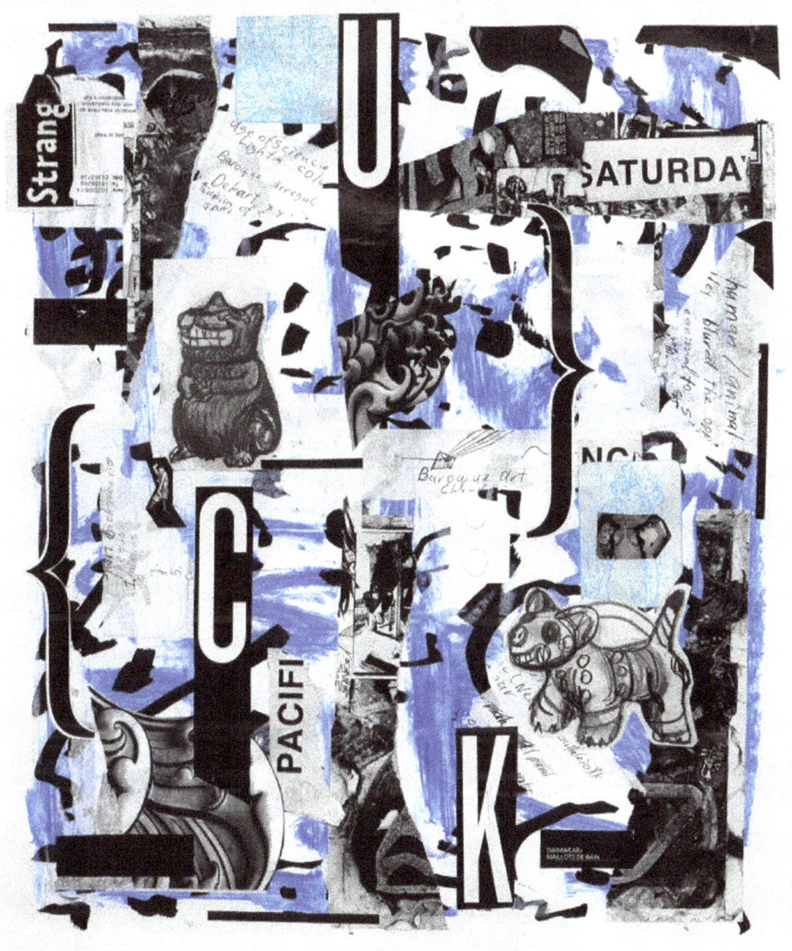

Luck

Chris Rekrutiak, 2020
Mixed Media on Paper
56cm x 66cm

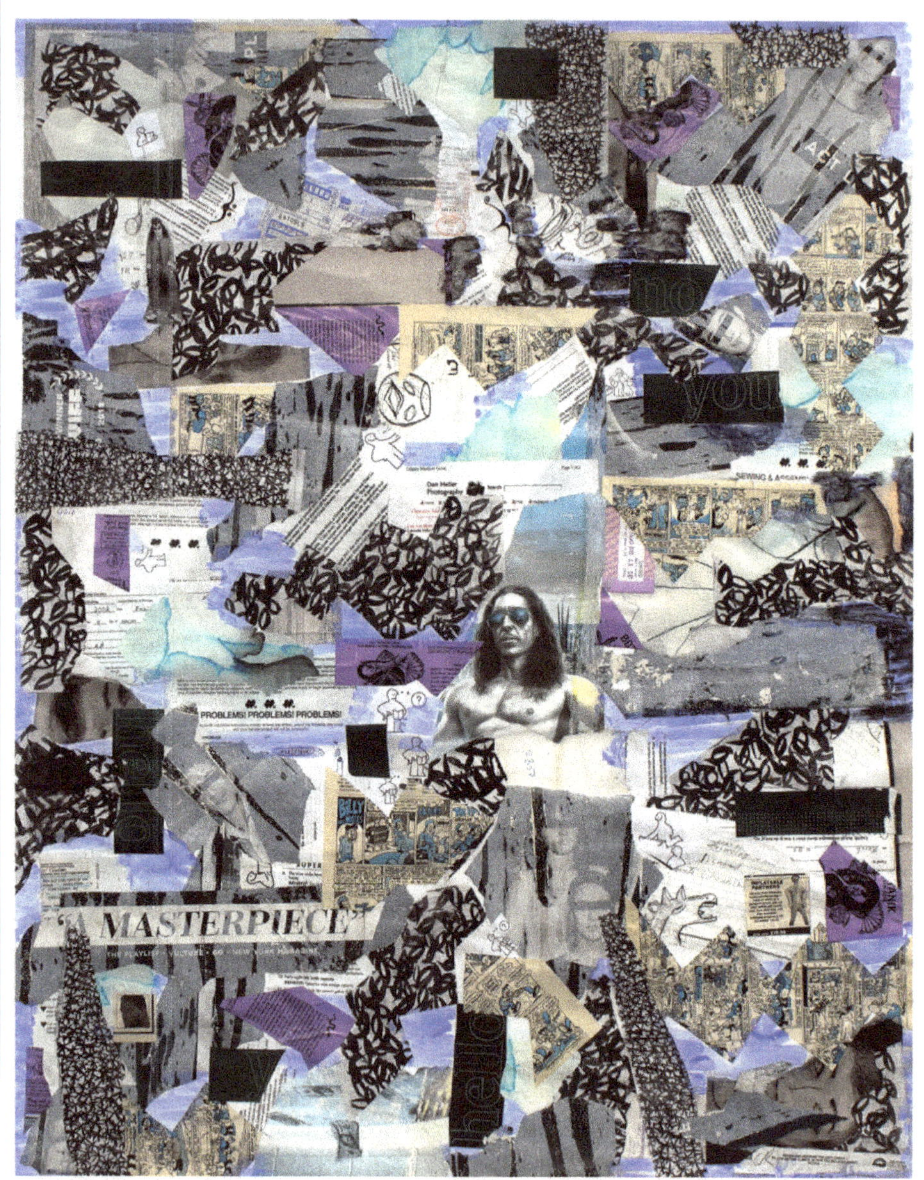

Homo-poisonous

Chris Rekrutiak, 2020
Mixed Media on Paper
117cm x 94cm

Ode to Extinction Level Event

Andrew Last

Toppled trash cans stroke the parkways
We hunt with smoking tips.
In this food coma of late modernity,
Revived mammoth caulks the menu.
Yet, gasping, winter threatens
    Our social distances
With x-ray visions of slipped discs,
    Long nights spent aspirating ministers.
Waking to throated tubes and nodules,
We rub white noise from family portraits.

All risk is existential by degrees,
Hence this protracted search for survivors.
We must protect the body clock at all costs,
The corporate structure of fire.
We are yet to transubstantiate a soul we didn't like.
    Misdiagnosed with heartburn, chests clutched,
We dream the dream of the skateboarder, loose
    Subsistence. Novelty arising from spilt paint,
Tendrils slinking beneath the ice
Of triggered silence.

Native womxn clumped as clay
With mxn upon walls dancing by firelight:
Cuts folded, cloaks hooded,
Yesterday's chase scene already tradition.
Tell we no lies without droning
    Or passing out beneath storied skies.
Freedom proves all exits are graves,
    Yet we choose shelter, bed of feathers.
Enacting agency upon thrones of fever,
Learning muted speech of kings.

Timelines project mere mortality
Unless juiced with side of blade.
Hungry for tragedy, our only poet
Conceals gaps with clippings.
In our doomed igloo, each thought
    Shudders as a thrown propeller.
Only the flattened curve of history

Can keep the bent hourglass guessing.
Only pursed lips, perfect embouchure,
Can produce the knockout blow.

 It takes a president to let this play out.
Theatre wings, a ward-winning tumour.
Such *panna cotta* strata are solely for decoration,
Charting personal growth in water-logged beds.
We plaster walls, scratch surfaces,
        scrape livings. Let's call it square.
Let's call our relatives without fighting
        Or passing on final words, hard pass:
"If we didn't have anything nice to say,
We didn't say anything at all."

Witness to Yesterday

Greg Turlock

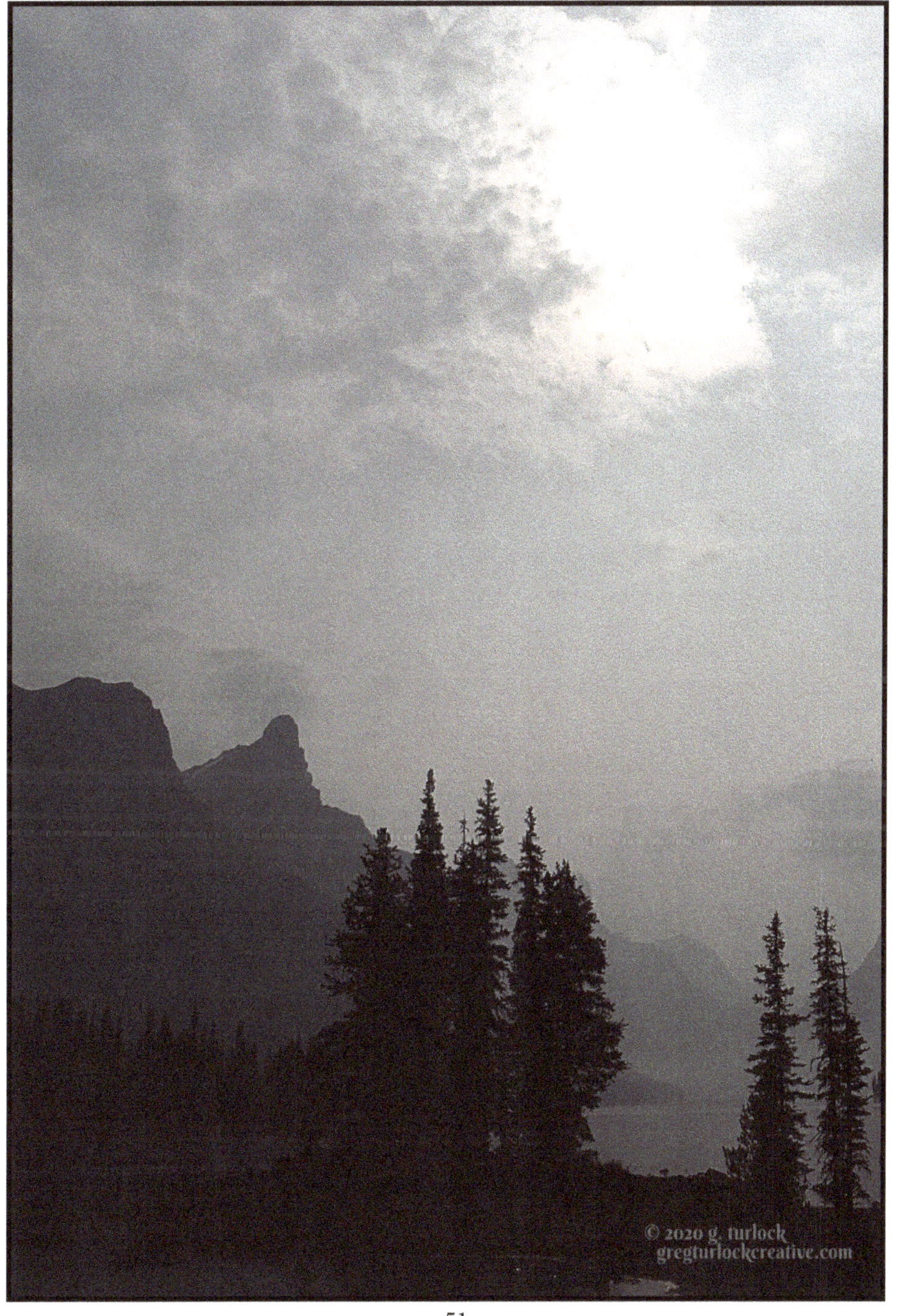

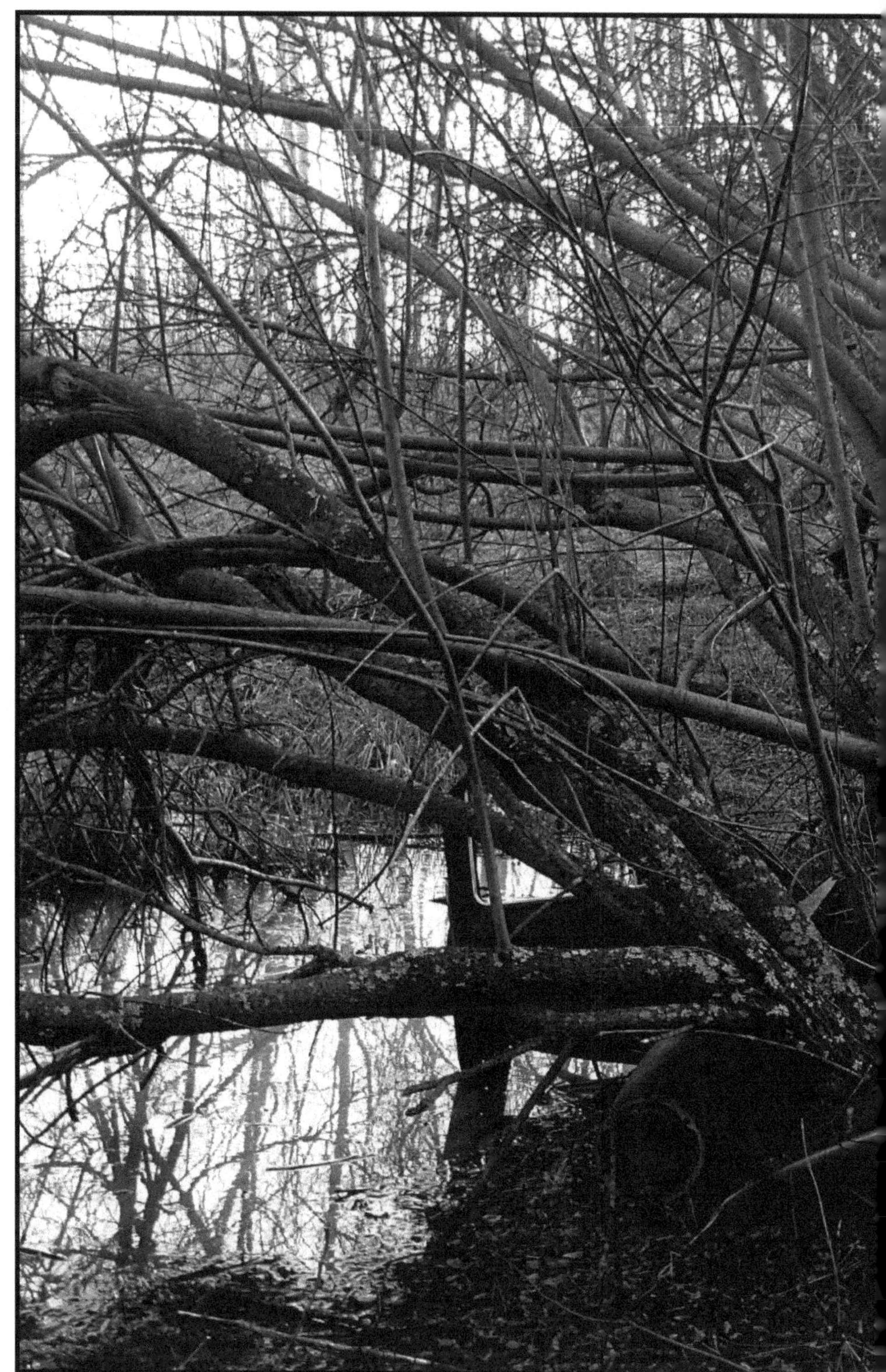

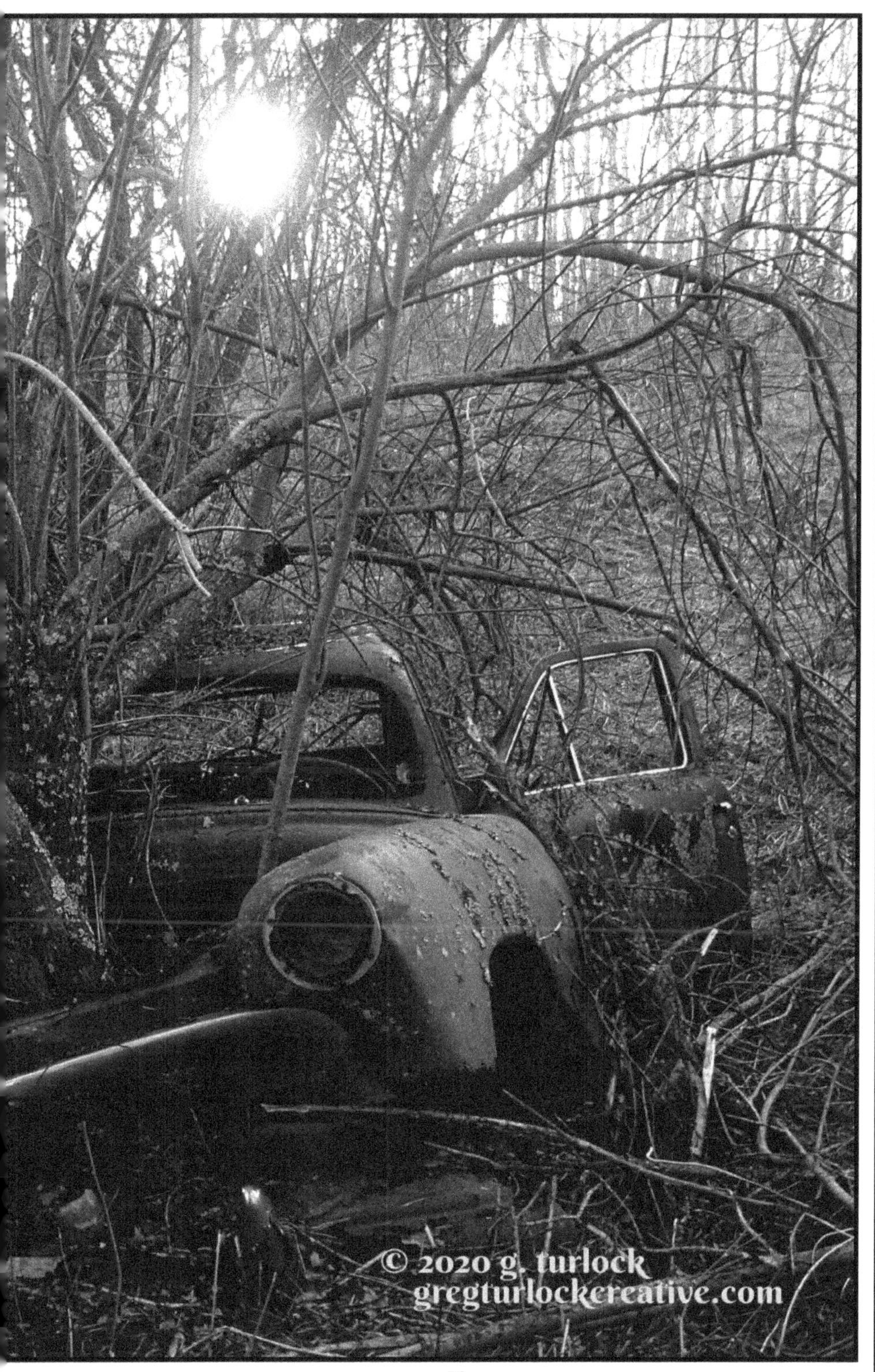
© 2020 g. turlock
gregturlockcreative.com

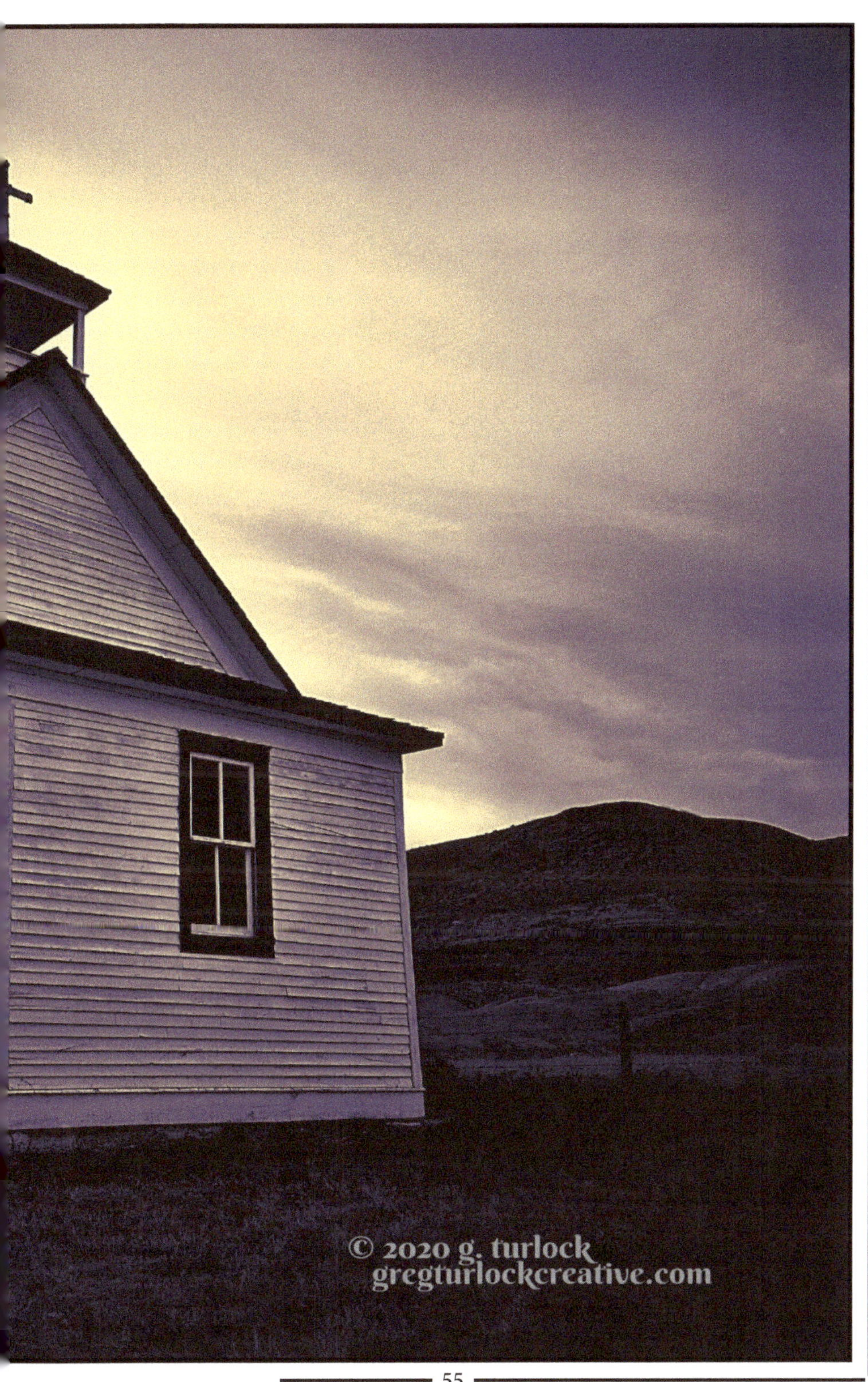

© 2020 g. turlock
gregturlockcreative.com

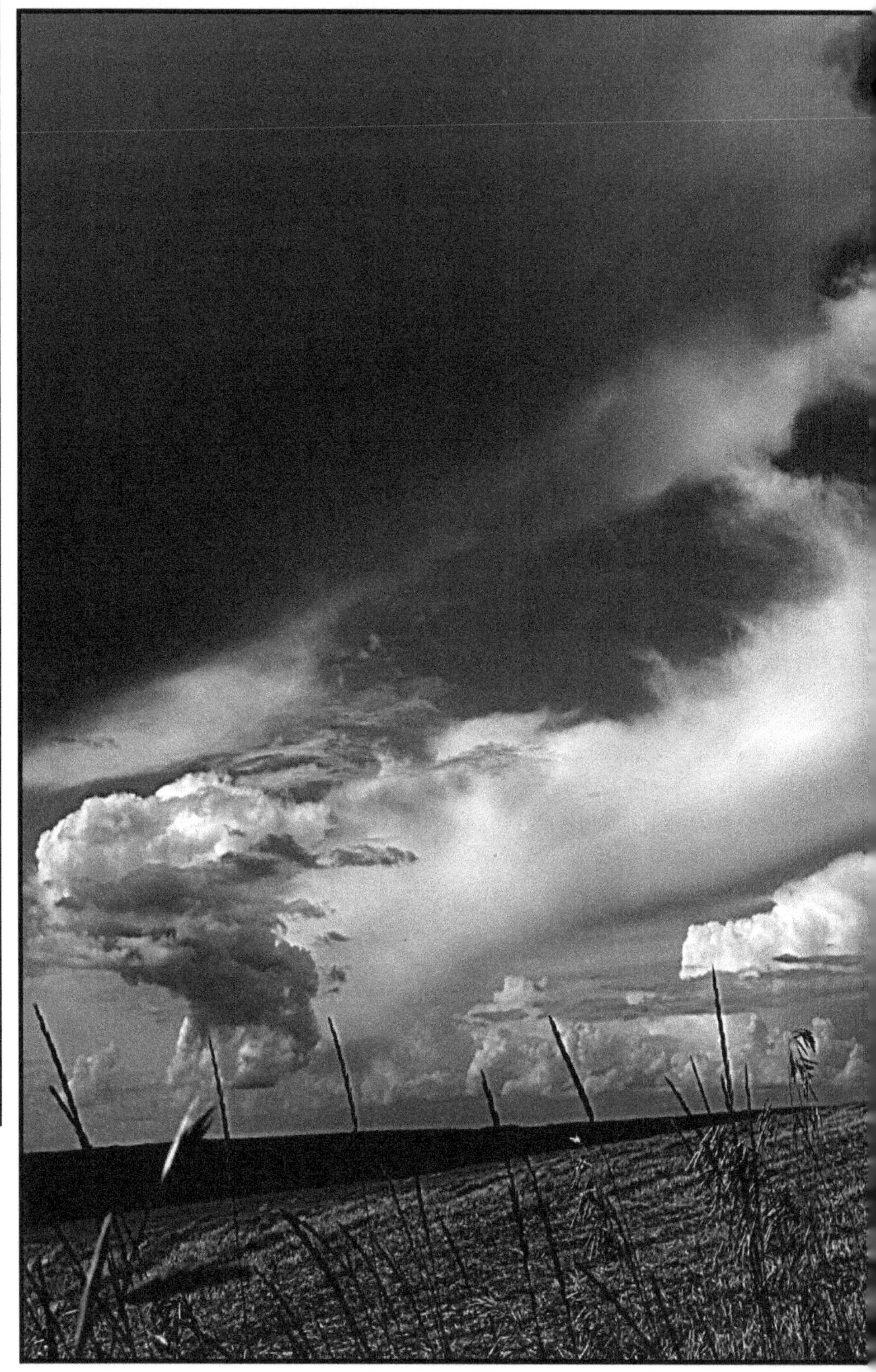

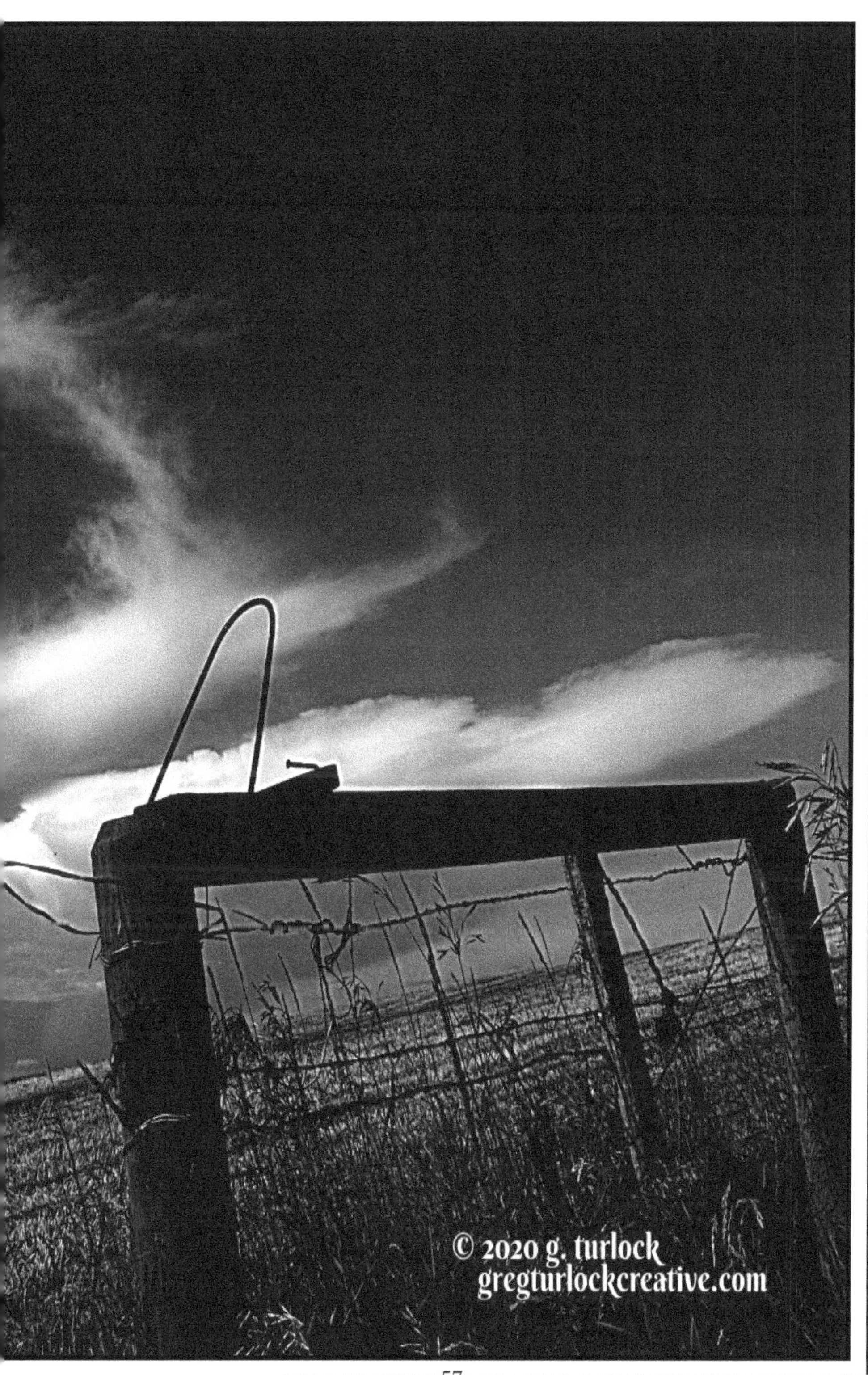
© 2020 g. turlock
gregturlockcreative.com

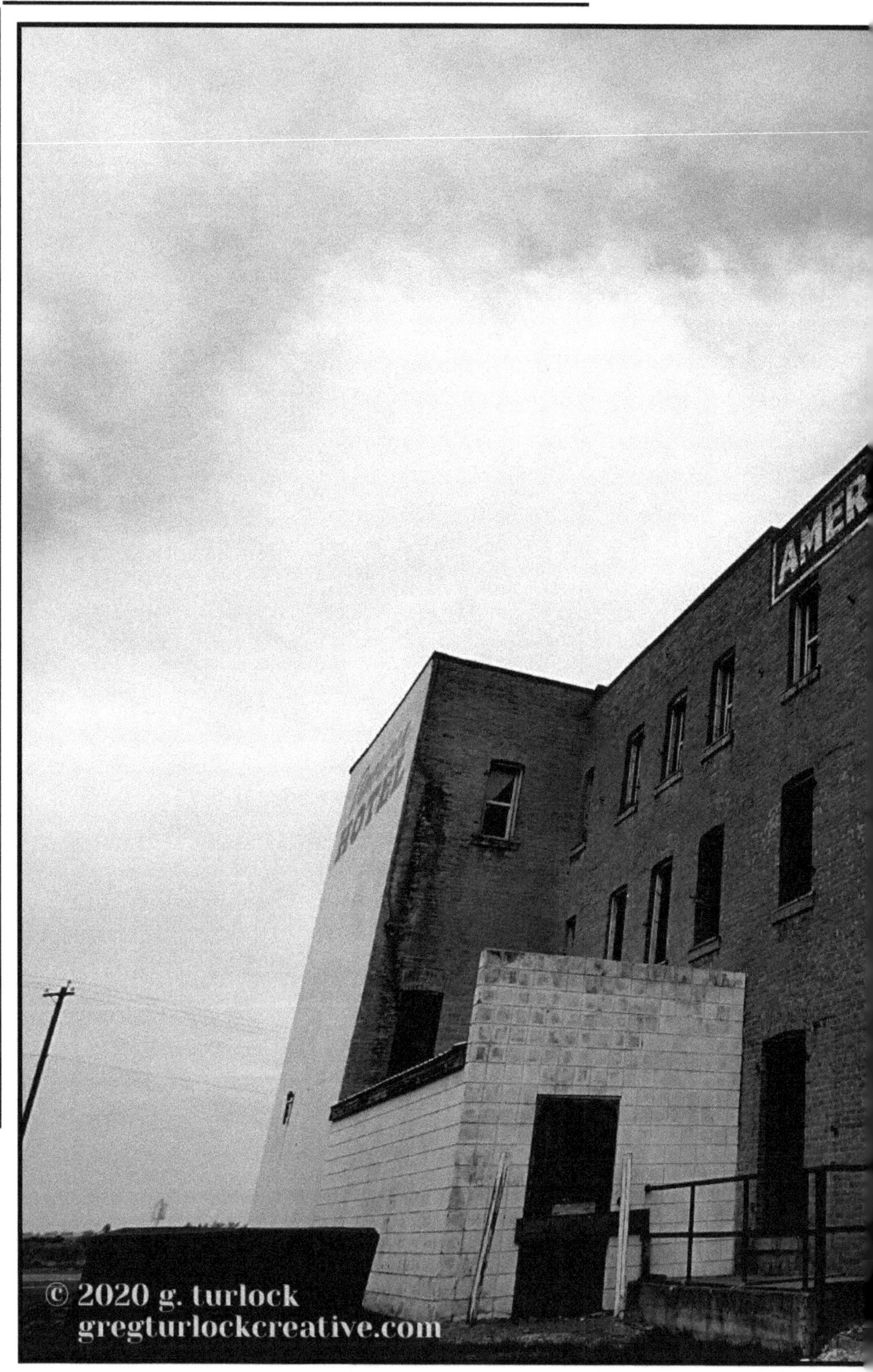

AMER
HOTEL
© 2020 g. turlock
gregturlockcreative.com

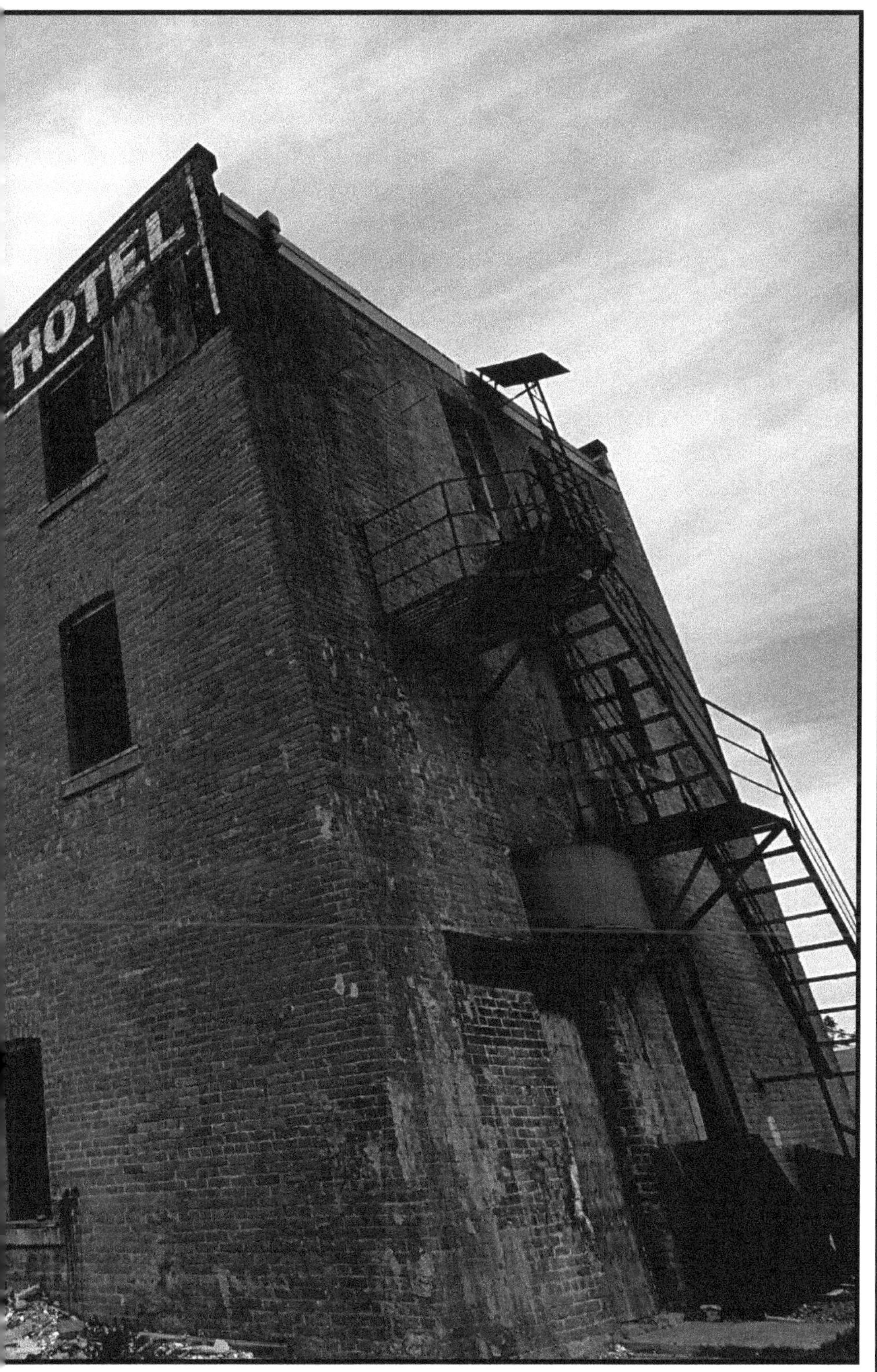
HOTEL

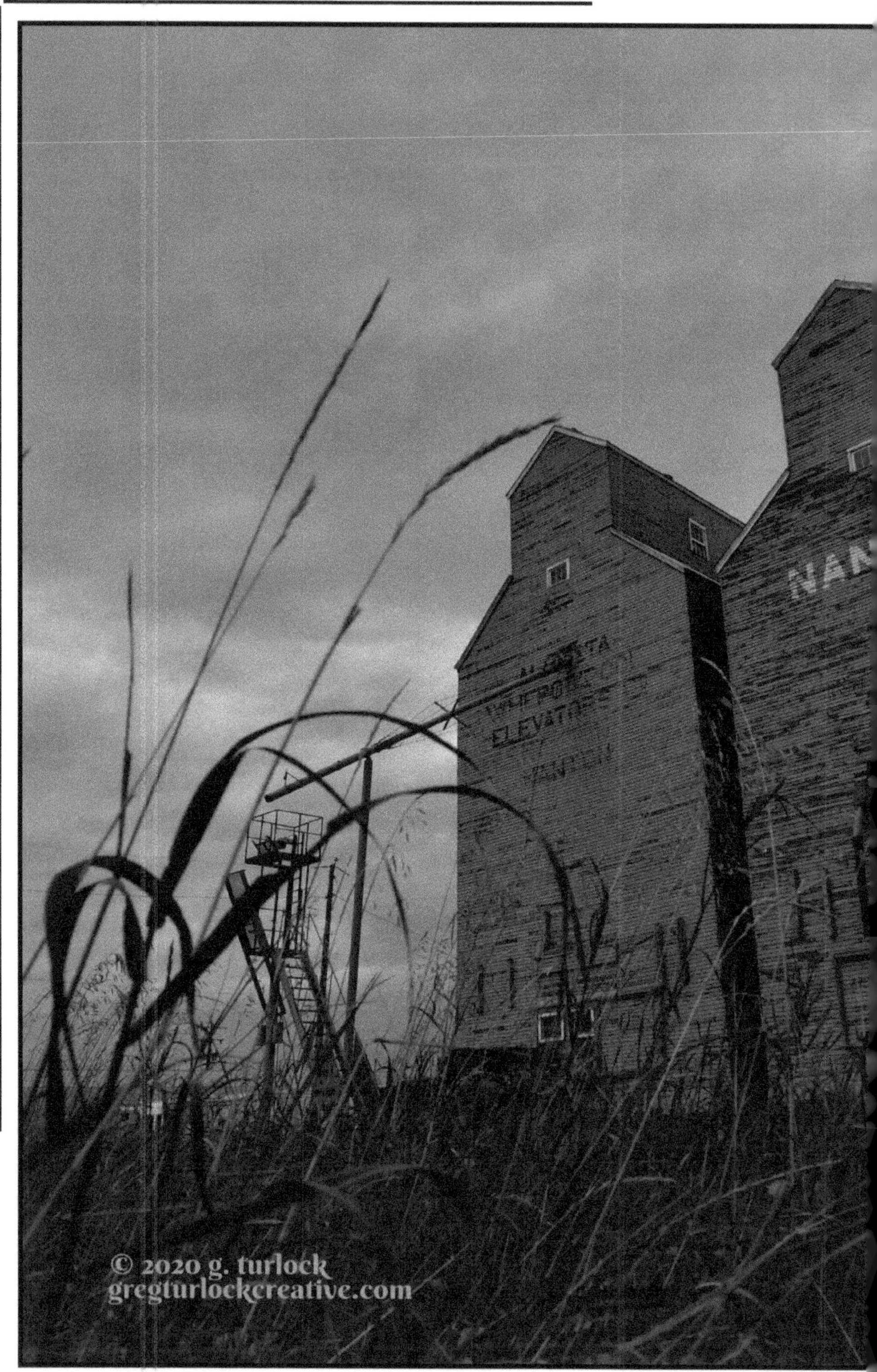

NAN
ALBERTA
WHEAT POOL
ELEVATOR
NANTON

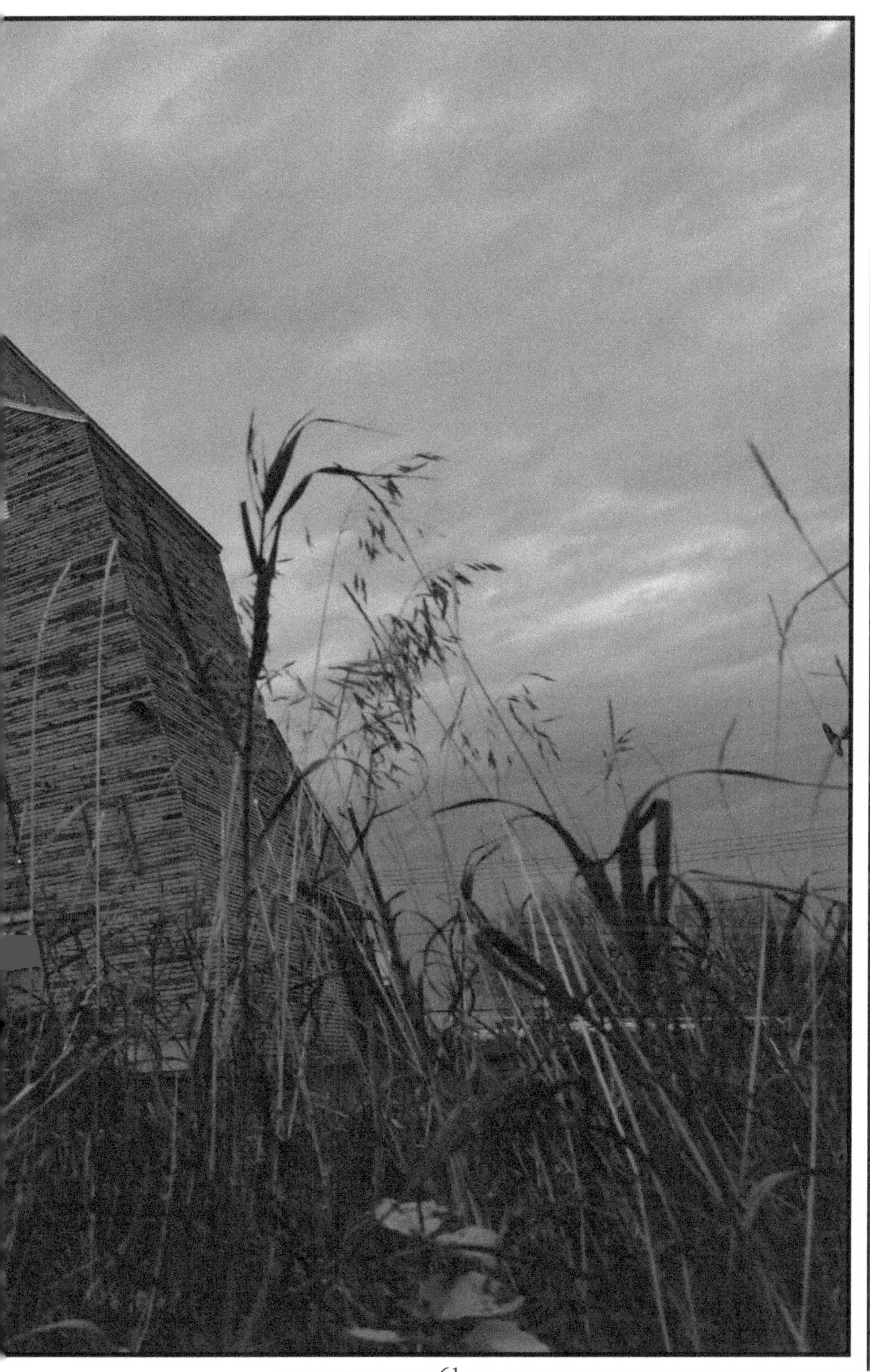

Manhattan Parks

Edward O. Byrne

Fragile the sparrow thin bones of his chest
  as a bundle of toothpicks and newspaper
  in hand with isosceles mouth
bleats a few syllables before departure
kindest the words that fall
                from his beak

wisp roads he'll travel orphaned from their purpose
on notes' wing return to me
as in sleep or riverless
       the montage of film

Hard to think what
significance
they could have
Hard to dream

arrowful path
to the arrowhead burial

  as from the abbey window
   robin hood flings his breath to the waiting ground
& finds the place
he lies forever in
         how we race
          toward the end of worldlines
         how we walk

& eye a lens
  sensitive to what
separates the not there
          and the there is
  beholds this peace
its grey tranquility
as the black-and-white photograph
the mind seeks to occupy
left out are the thousand identical street corners
bricks stacked to the pavement
will never hear songs such as this

how silence today tends to deafen
& grow   how absence

THE HOUSE ON GEOLOGIC SEPARATIONS

Mike Perez

There's this sanded myth that we are half
a unity. a proto-continent that every cell in
our body is drawn *to, by and from*—I call it
an old Pangaeaic ache that every new love reenacts
each night when spooning against your chest,

their back like the arc of Africa against the firm
fleshed coastline of your severed Americas.
Where we are whole and free and one at once.
Nice work if you can get it. Geology has worked

without us, grifting, churning, spiraling in plumes
its hoarded liquid fires, linked back to a core
of unrelenting violence. So what. If inhuman
instincts metamorphose to a fault, I sense an
unbearable tectonics, not at my feet, but in air.

This is a tectonics that must travel restlessly.
The aftermath of separations aired, long-stored
in our bodies' mimetics. Where all I did was rage
against a man who formed on his own, and split.

Because another man I loved too hard
has left in tremors, all my hands hold
after a break are sifted absences, in shocks.
The day he left a sort of morning-after

science dawned, older than all cliffs or capes,
all crevices, all seams, all ruptures sealing

in reverse as I reached out again in light
to draw him close and he was gone; I walked
outside and looked around, what land was this,

so free? I was whole and floating, self-contained.
I survived myself. Now what, stopped mid-morning drift?
The break was everything in that it shaped
me not in reference to him, but to my limits—

haunted by ancient severances, thrusting
away at him caving to my enacted strike-slip faults,
the retroactive friction as I tried to start a ruckus
or fuck, reviving the tethered start that formed my own

firm private Florida. To heal, we must start,
embrace wherever land first landed in the
union of our cells to build our inaugural
landing. Where could I go but backward, to

my parent's old house on the beach,
the Fernandina Beach house on the North end
where they met in 1949, where I brought
the fled love just two months ago

to meet the folks. We fought all day
and loved all night. My mother said, *He's
not the one.* He always said, *You're never
where your feet are. Please check in.* Okay.

Today the beach has more than sifted rhetoric:
the tide has left jetsamed corsages
of moss and shells for a shotgun marriage

in sand and foam; an ibis combs its natural plot
with beaks like patient, personal derricks on

the lawn next to the steps where my father
stood and held his bride in American love.
I still have eyes: there on the beach
there is a mother and her toddler digging
softly, I can still see that even geologic loss
built up as romance, war and ruin can re-build—that,
under siege, there is ablution and a dwelling:

there: I see the mother take her toddler's
bucket, flip it on his head: a wash of laughter
cleanses as she gathers that around her,
fist by fistful, and starts to dig a moat—
the strong caress of a waveless *in utero*
remembered—and says, *Here, where your feet are,*
is where and how you learn to make a house.

We can build on any severance, near or far, if
each speck coheres as if it were reconciled with
parent rock, part of a parted particle, building
from erosion—where the cling is everything—
a certain place where time goes back and forth,
amenable to being moved and holding in hard pauses.

Please hold me once again, my future fit, or in the
spectral clot of my parent revived to dwell in fertile dust.
More than just this broken legacy of ancient plates,
recast in us their common nightly union of met skin.
Keep us where we started, before we governed, seized,

and penetrated in a human name, embodying, inheriting

awareness as done, daily breakage, grant me—

love, land, parent—that a union's not a myth.

Covid Prints

Cynthia Yatchman

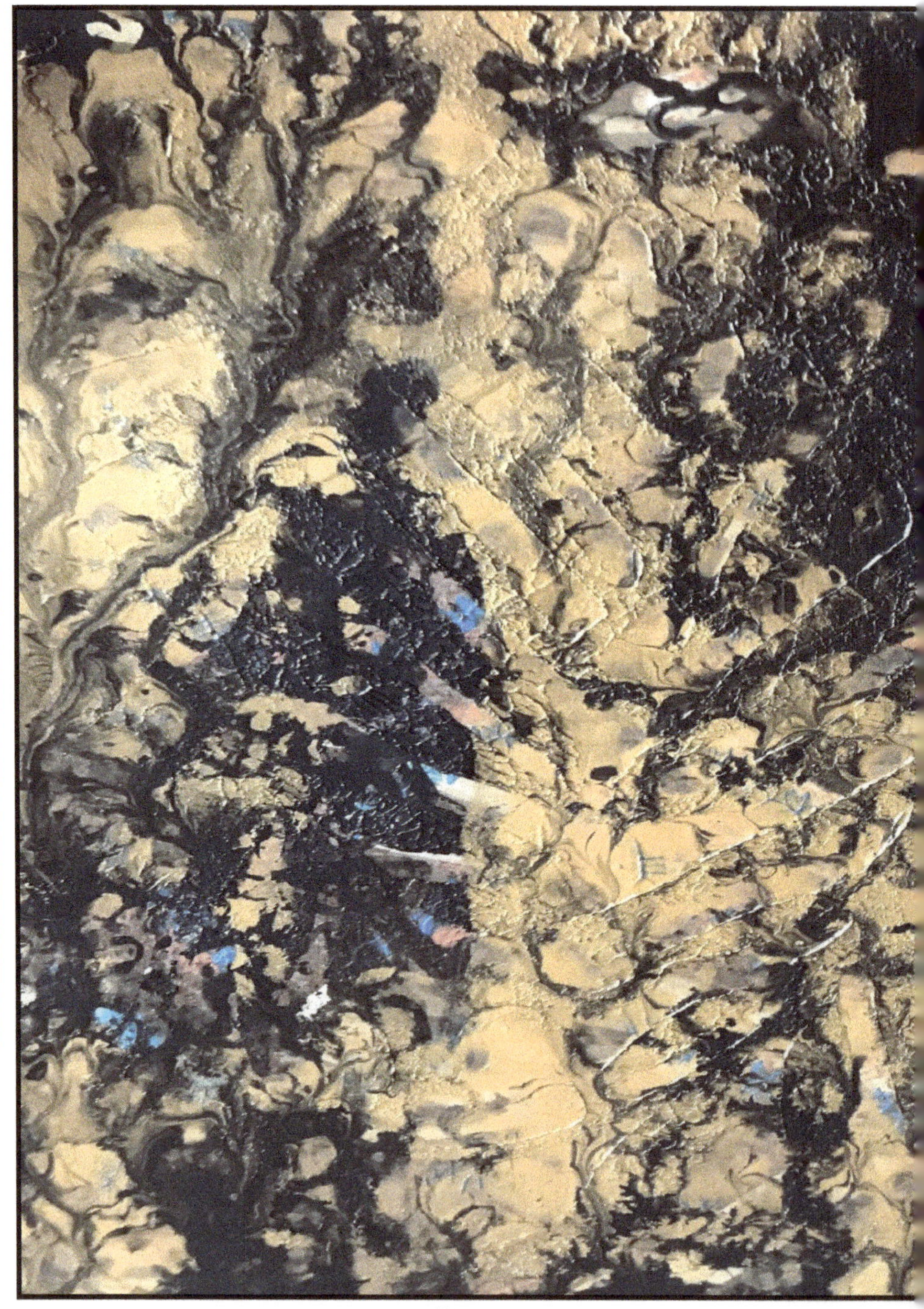

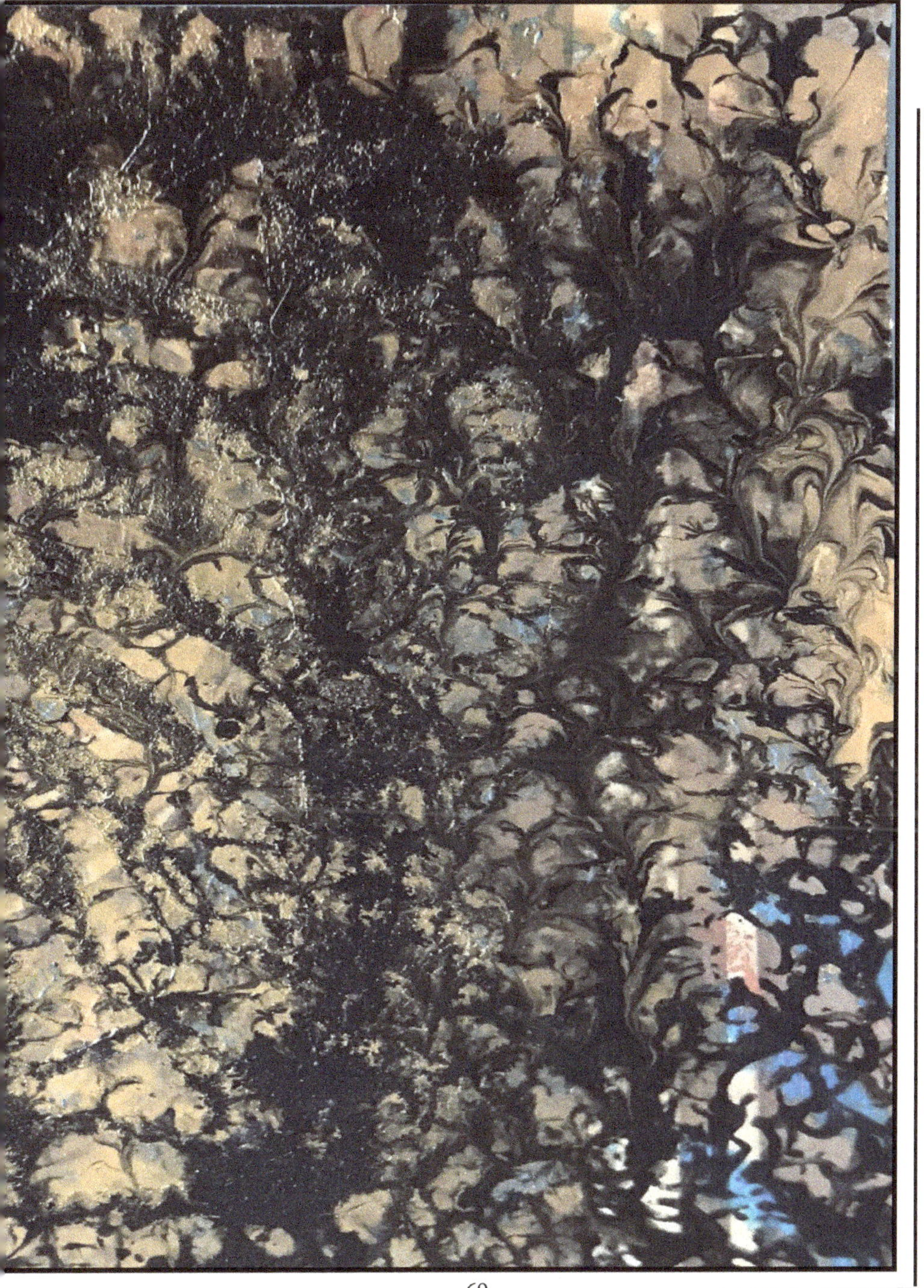

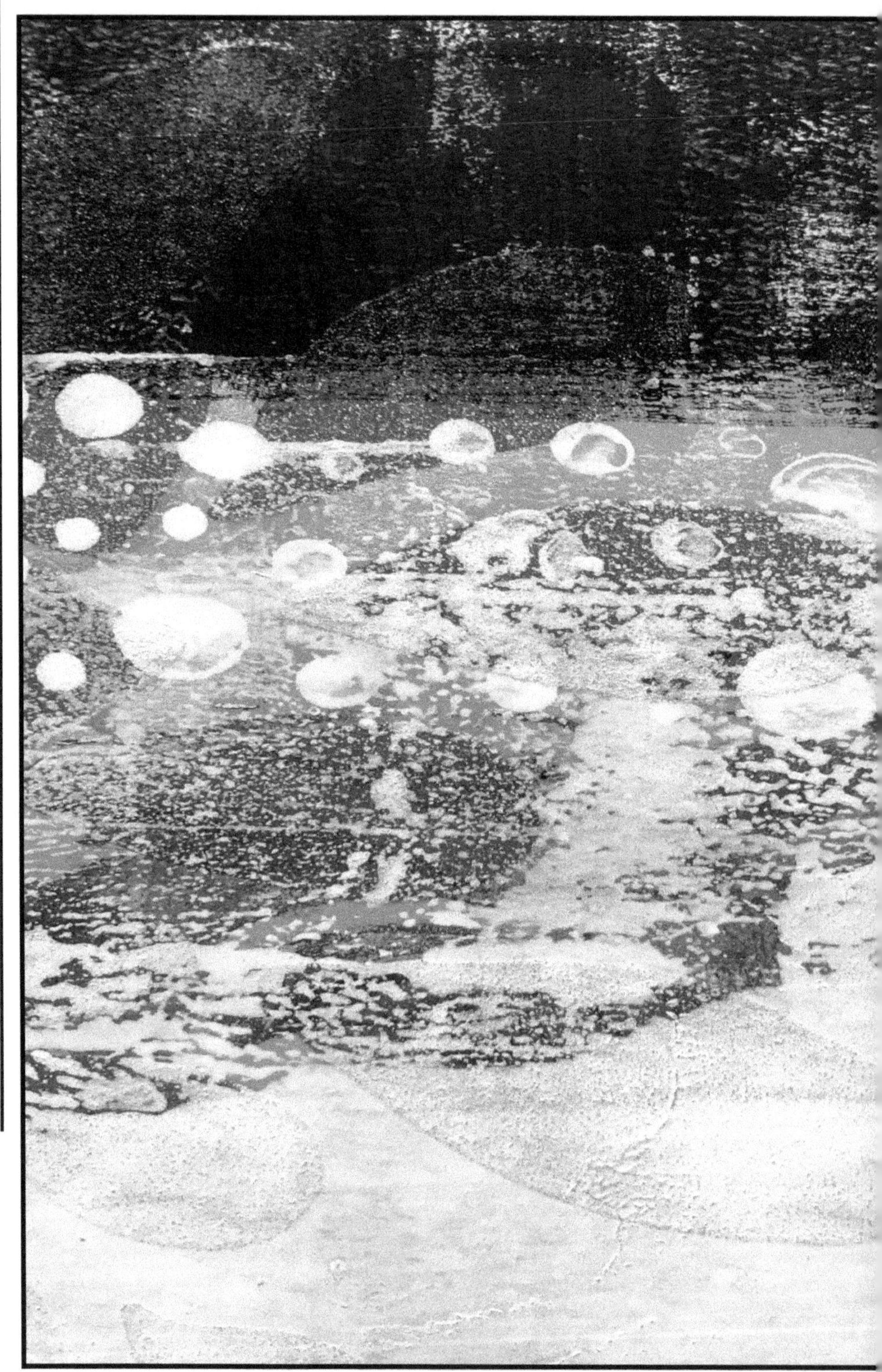

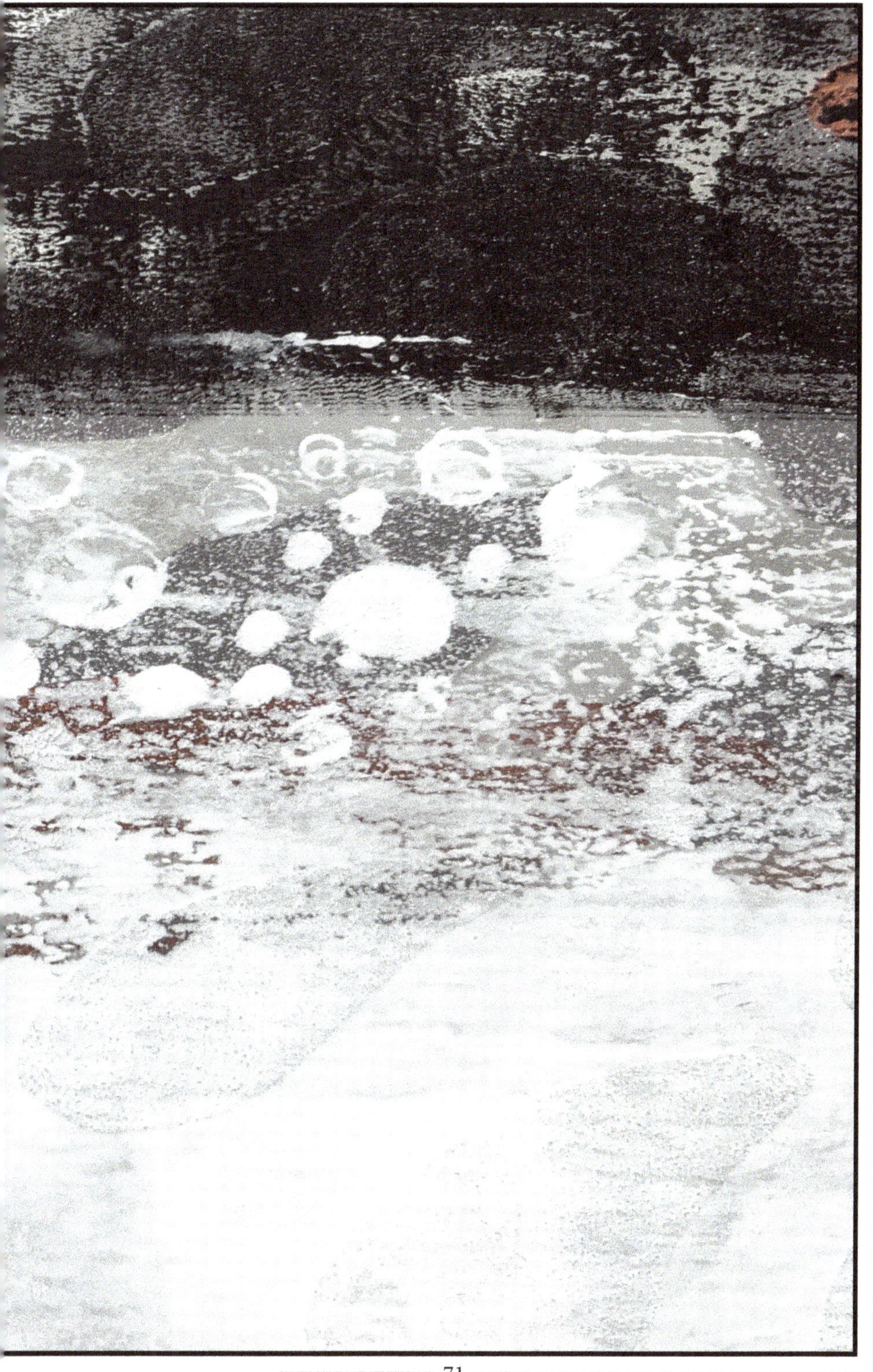

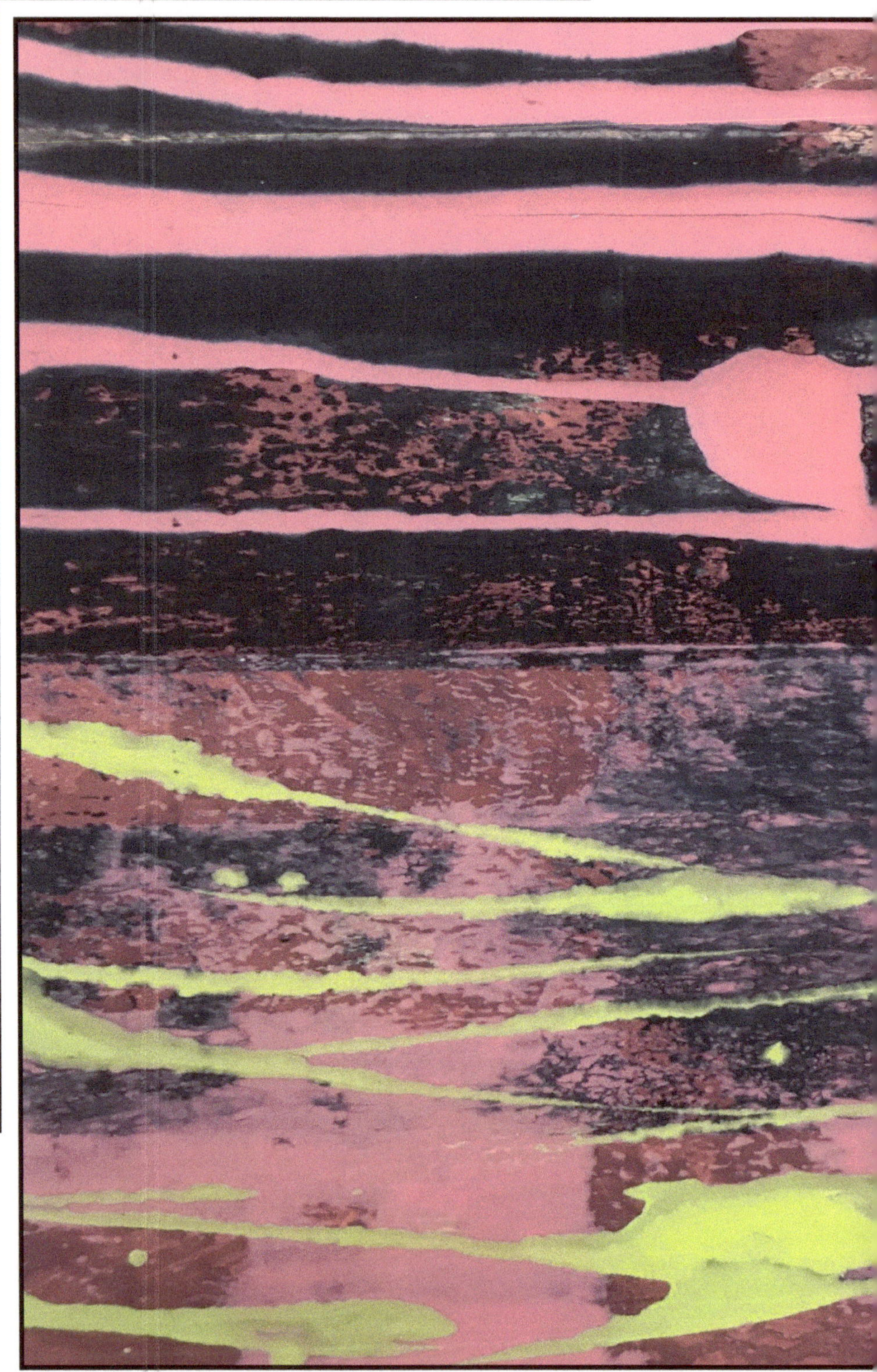

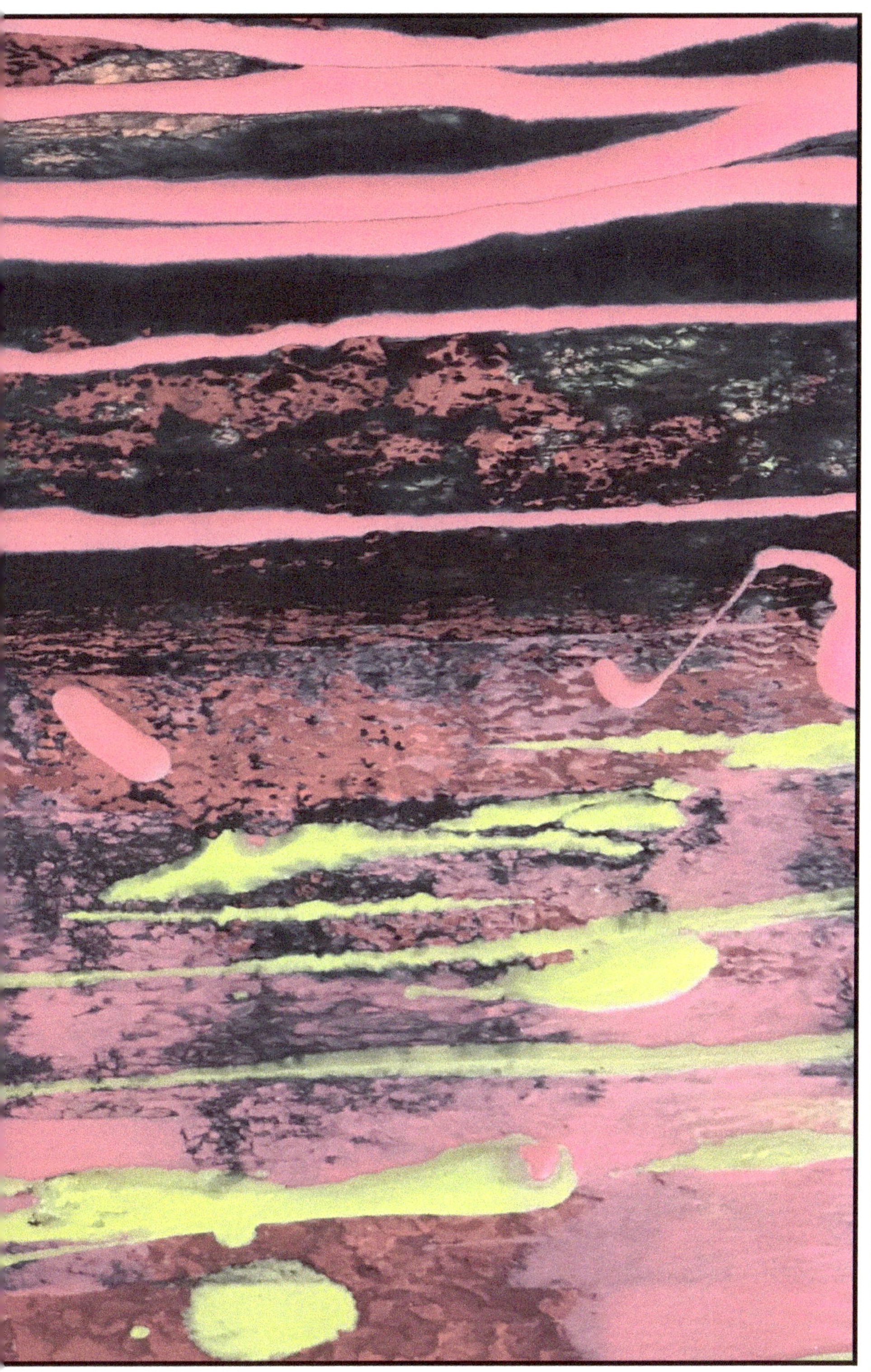

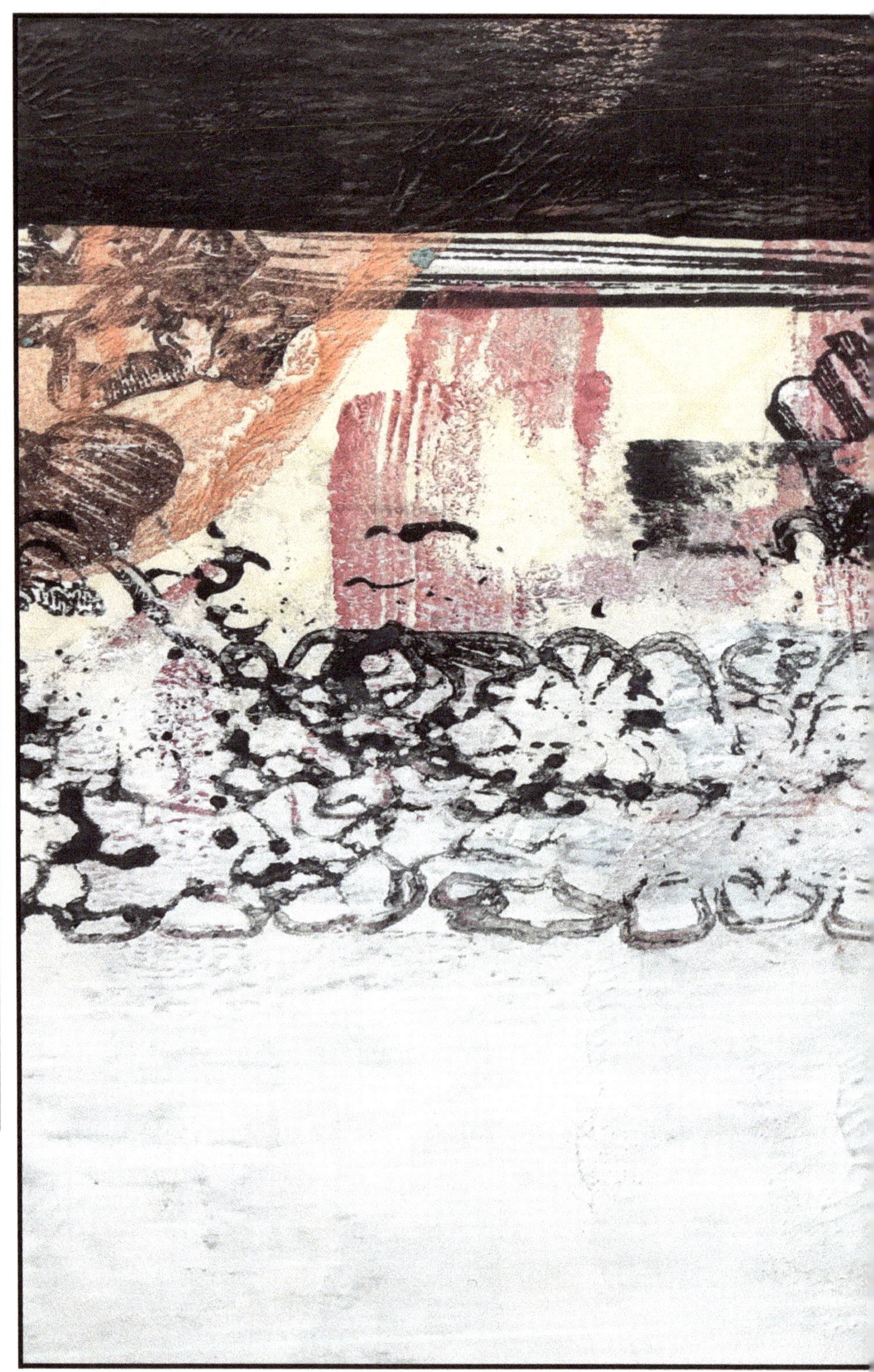

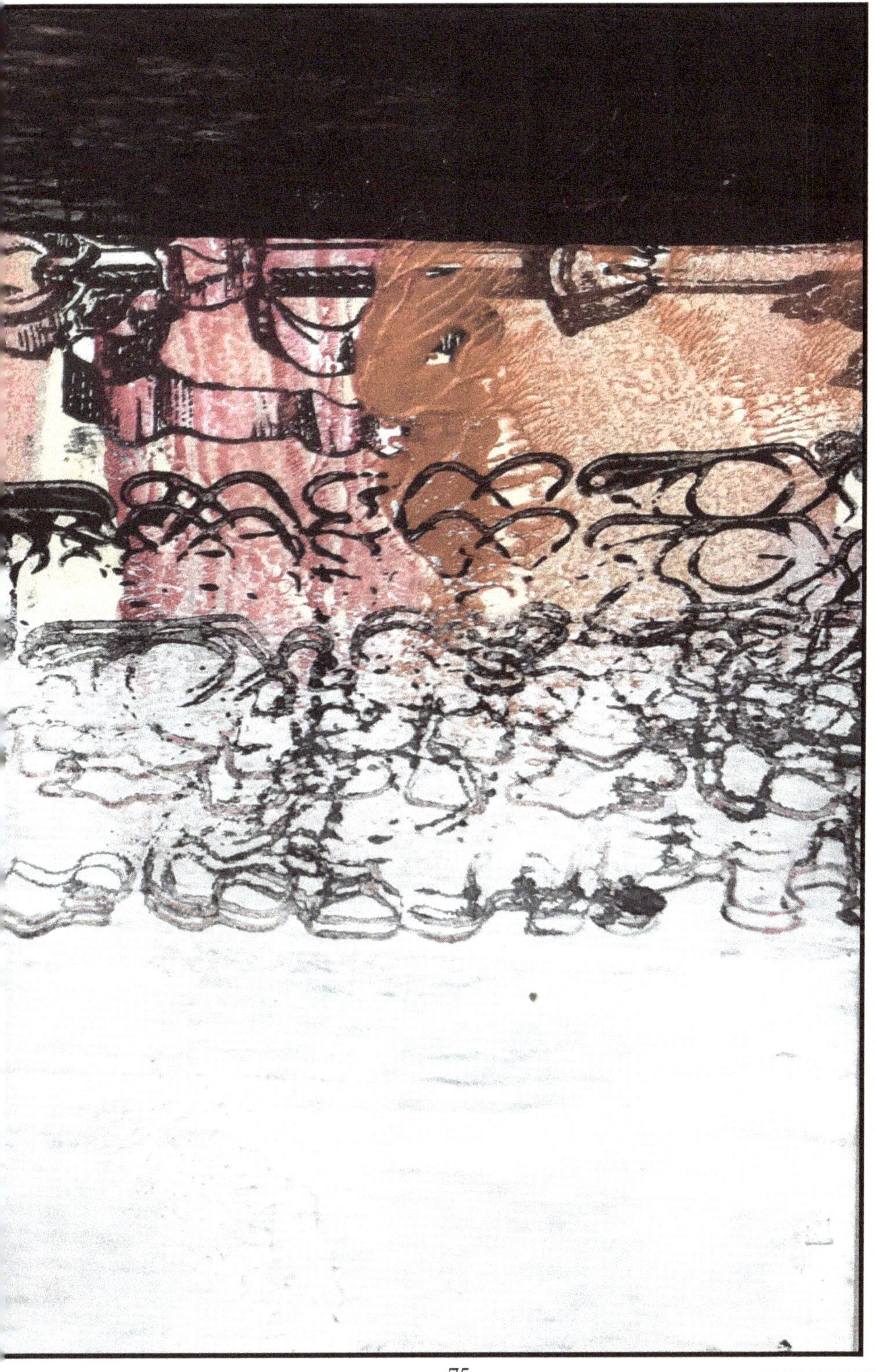

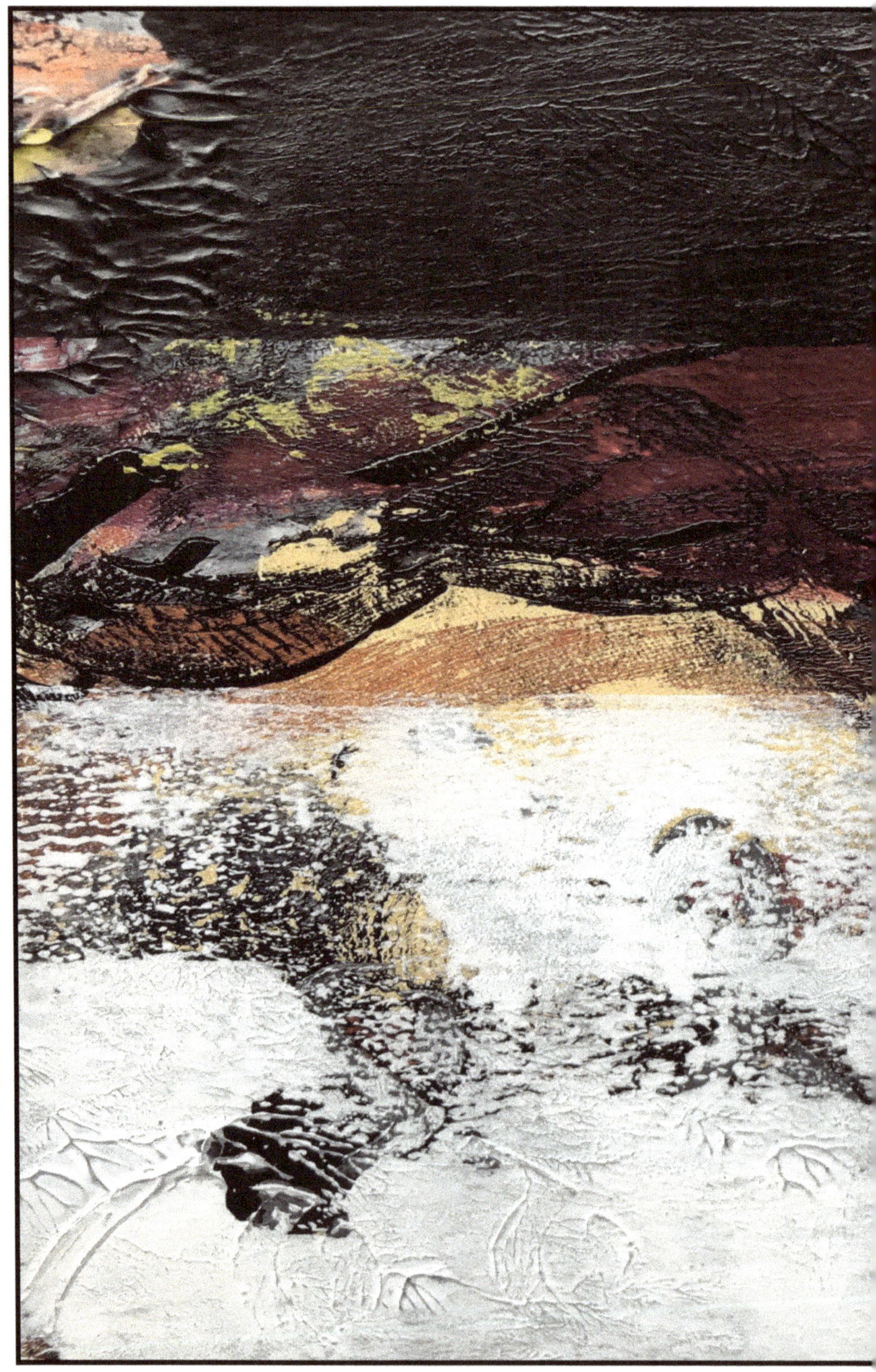

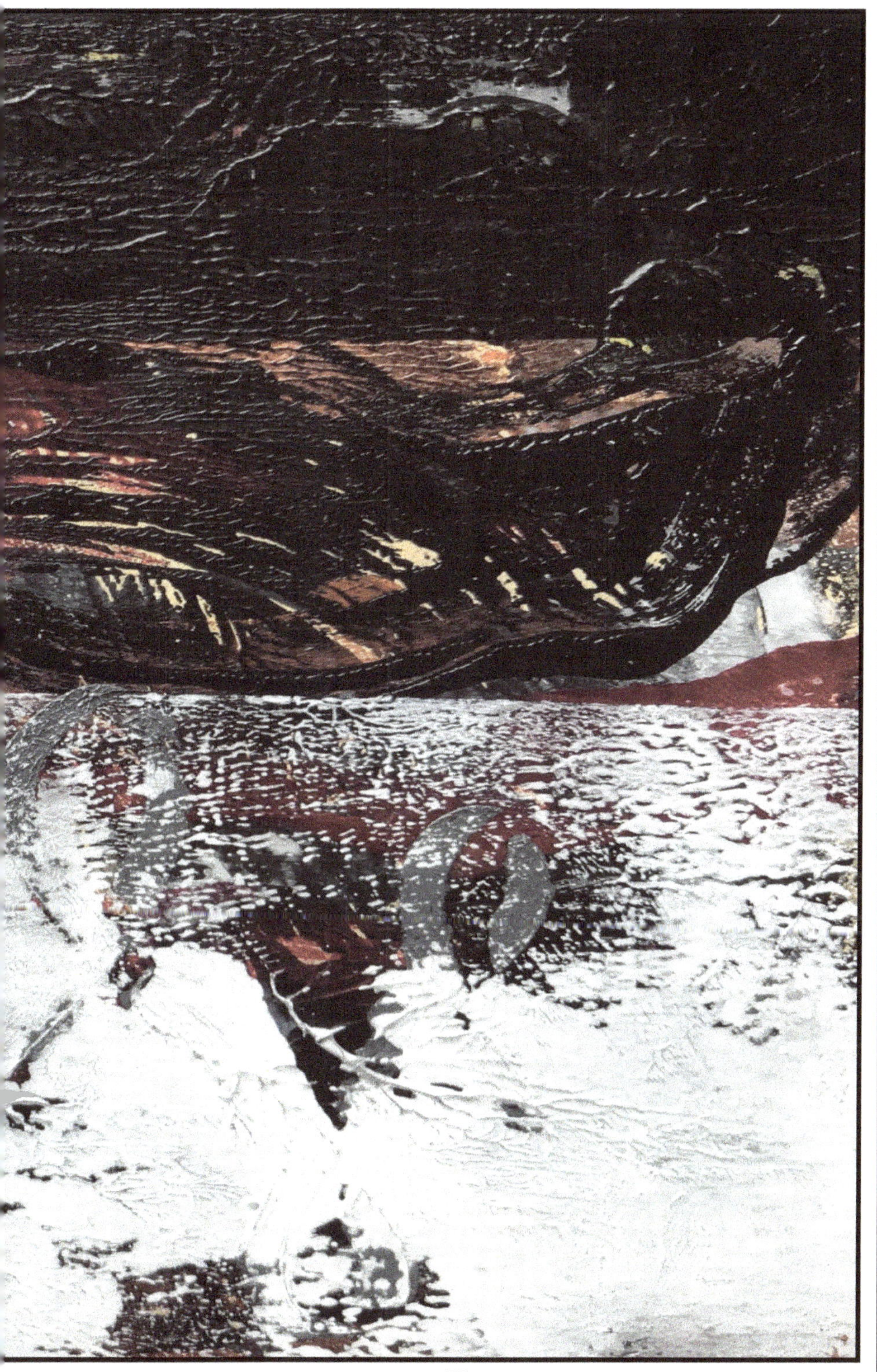

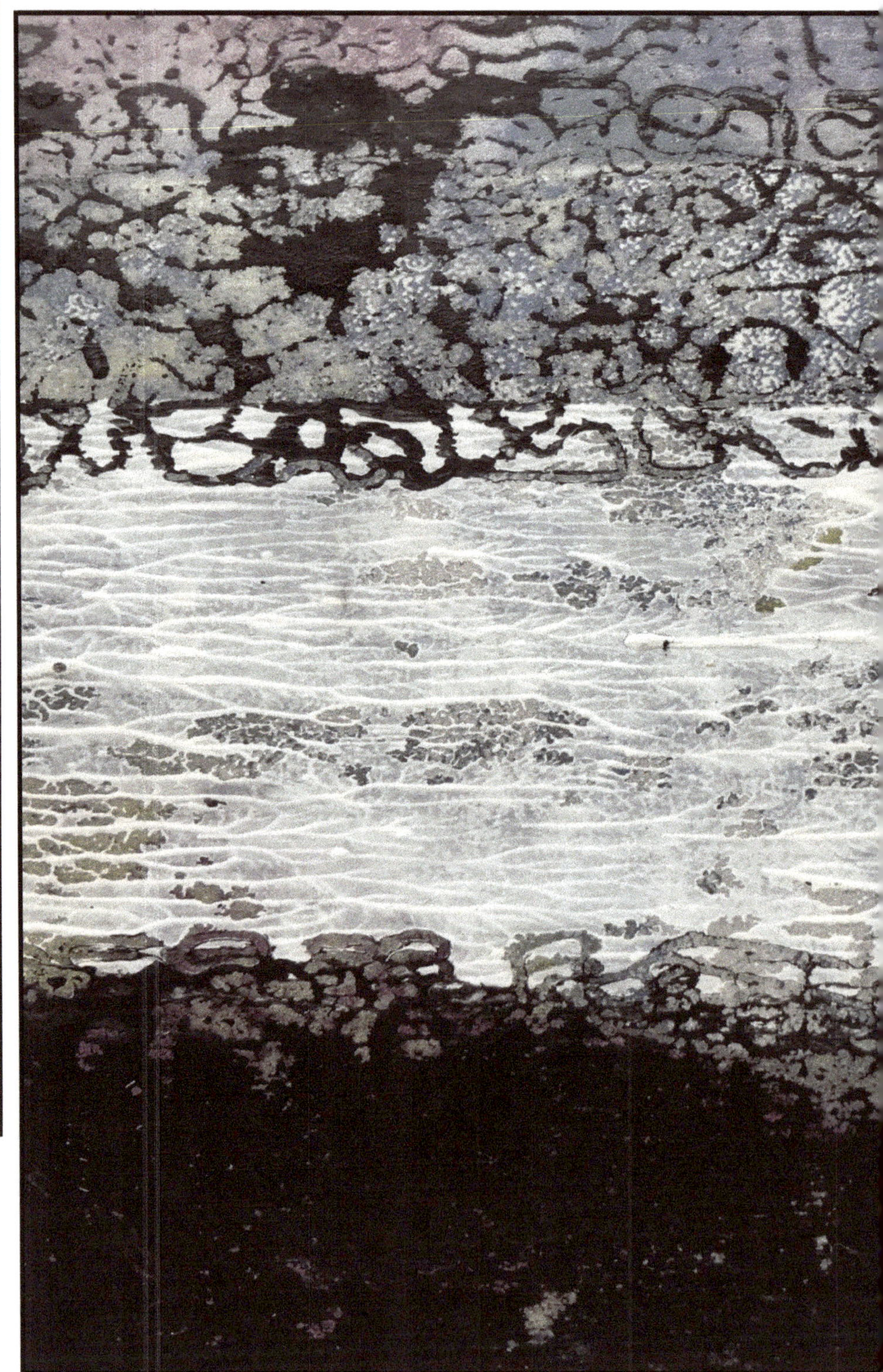

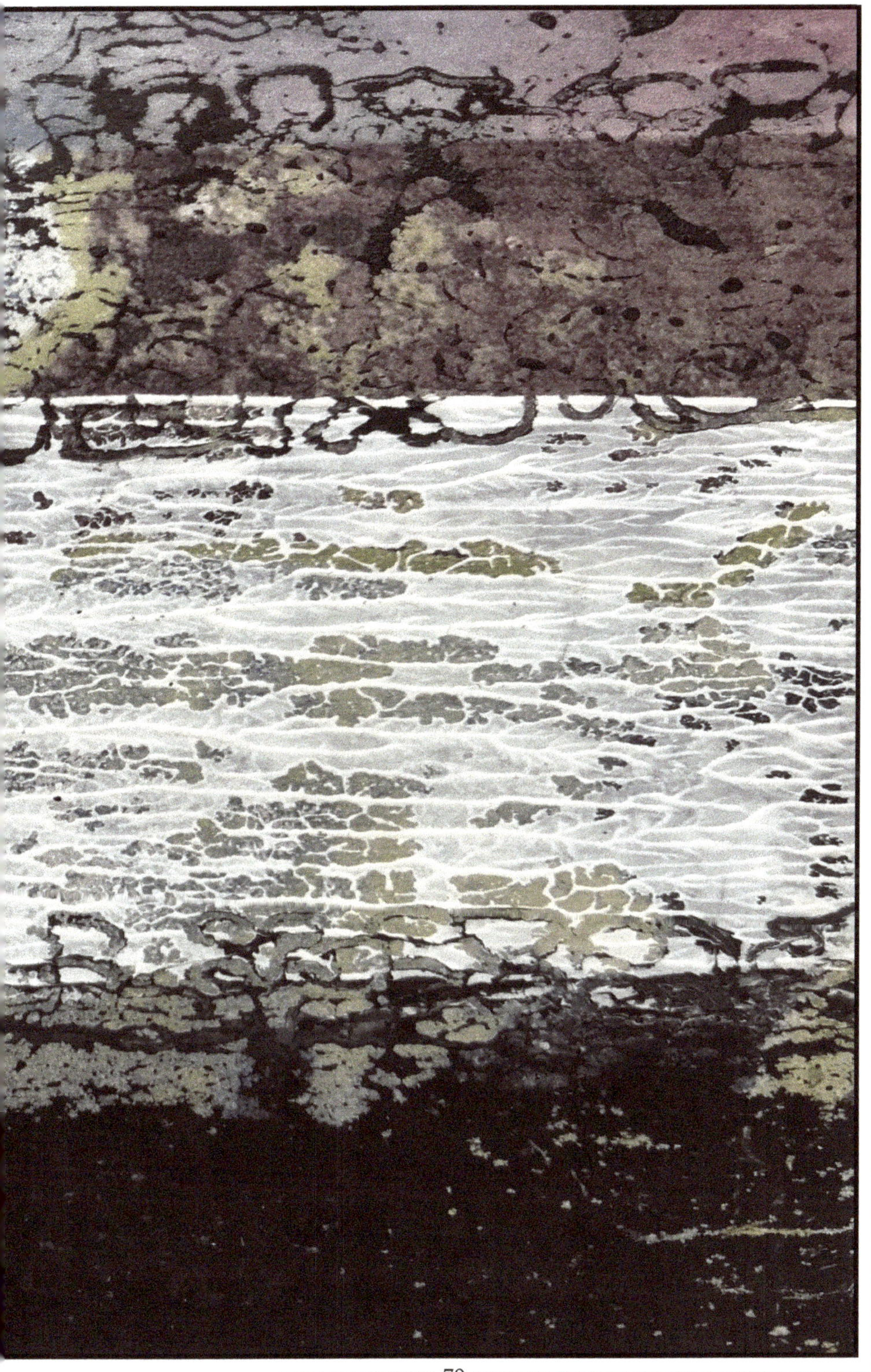

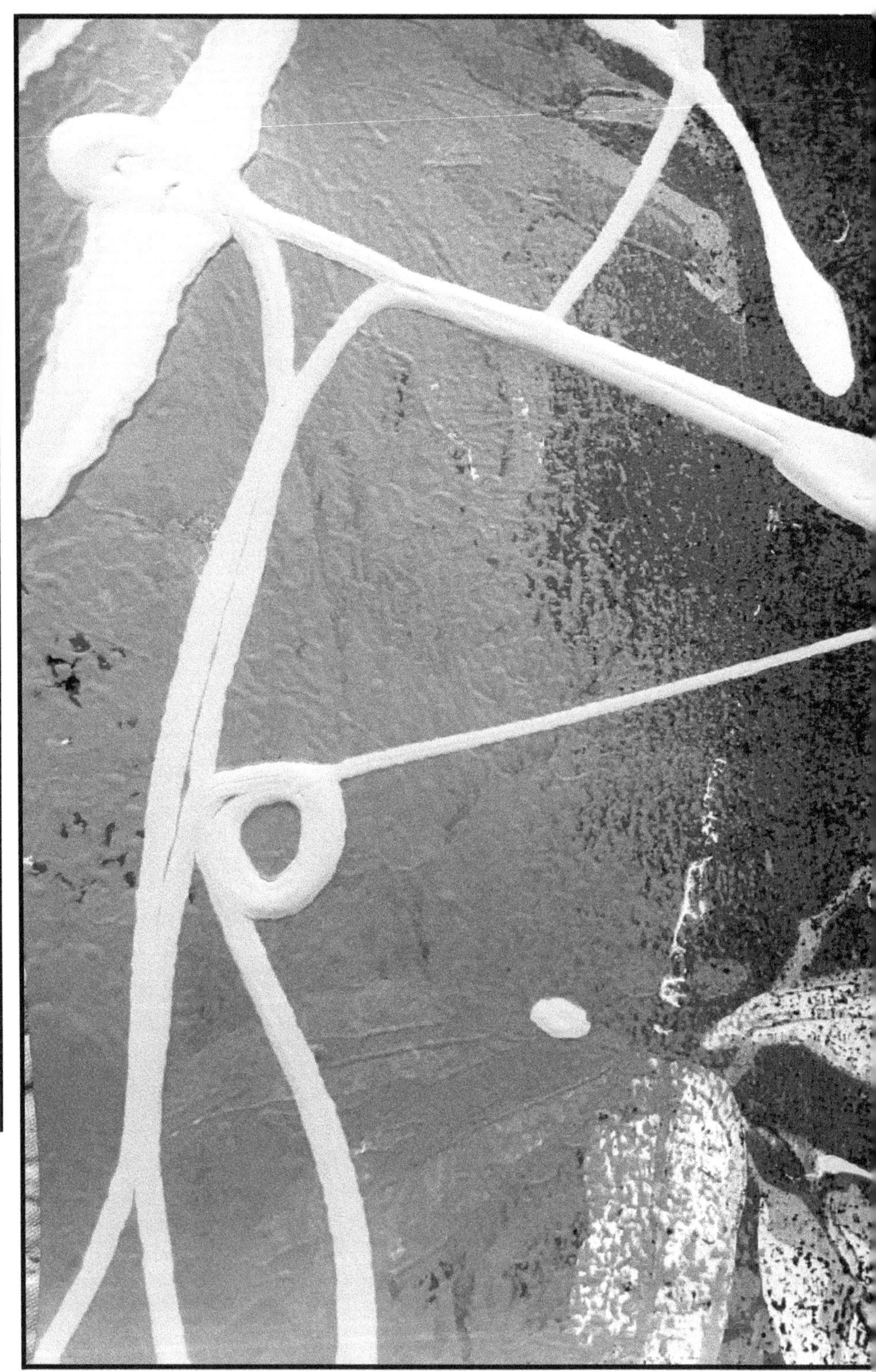

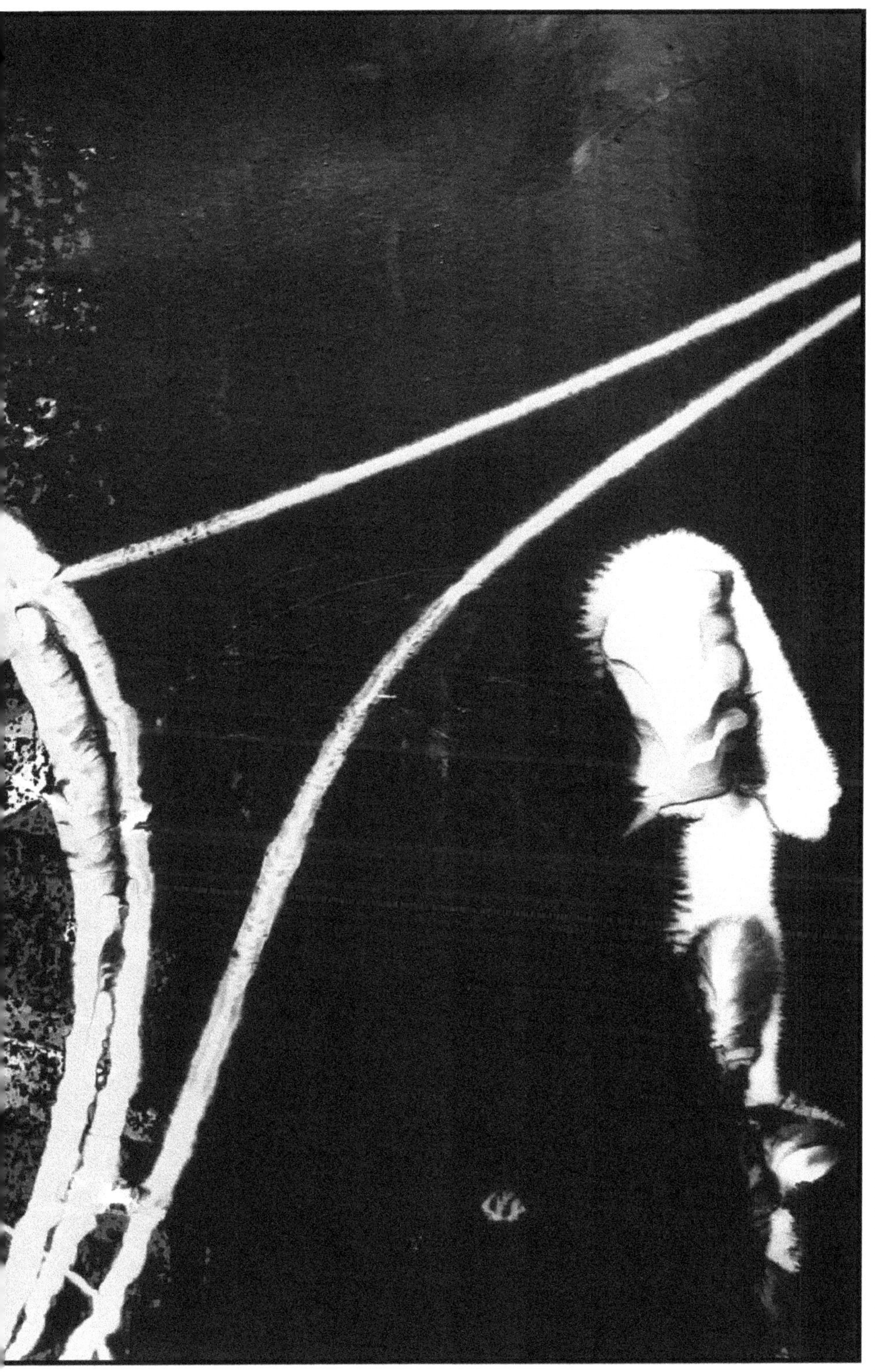

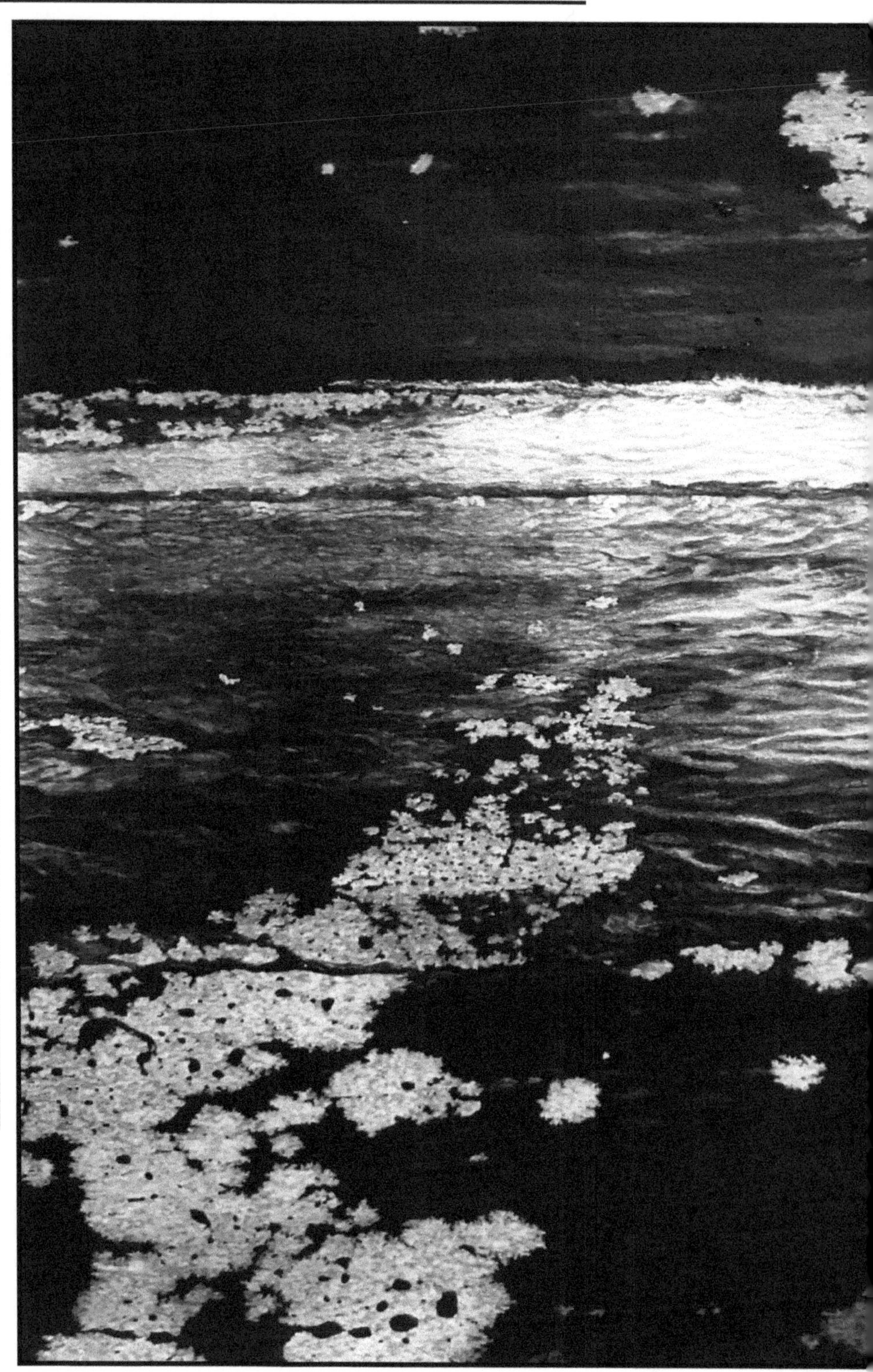

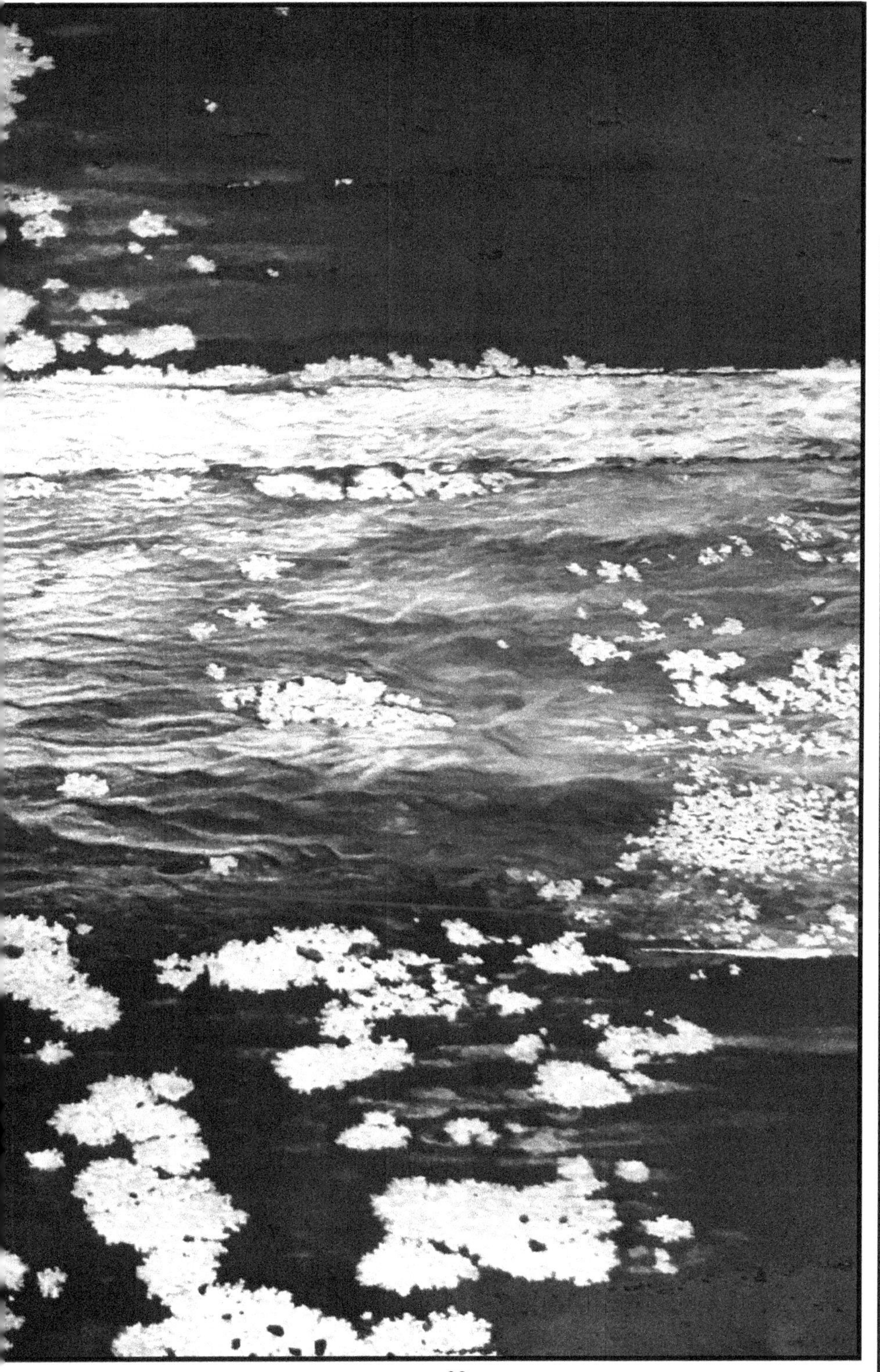

Strangers on the Subway

Nava Derakhshani

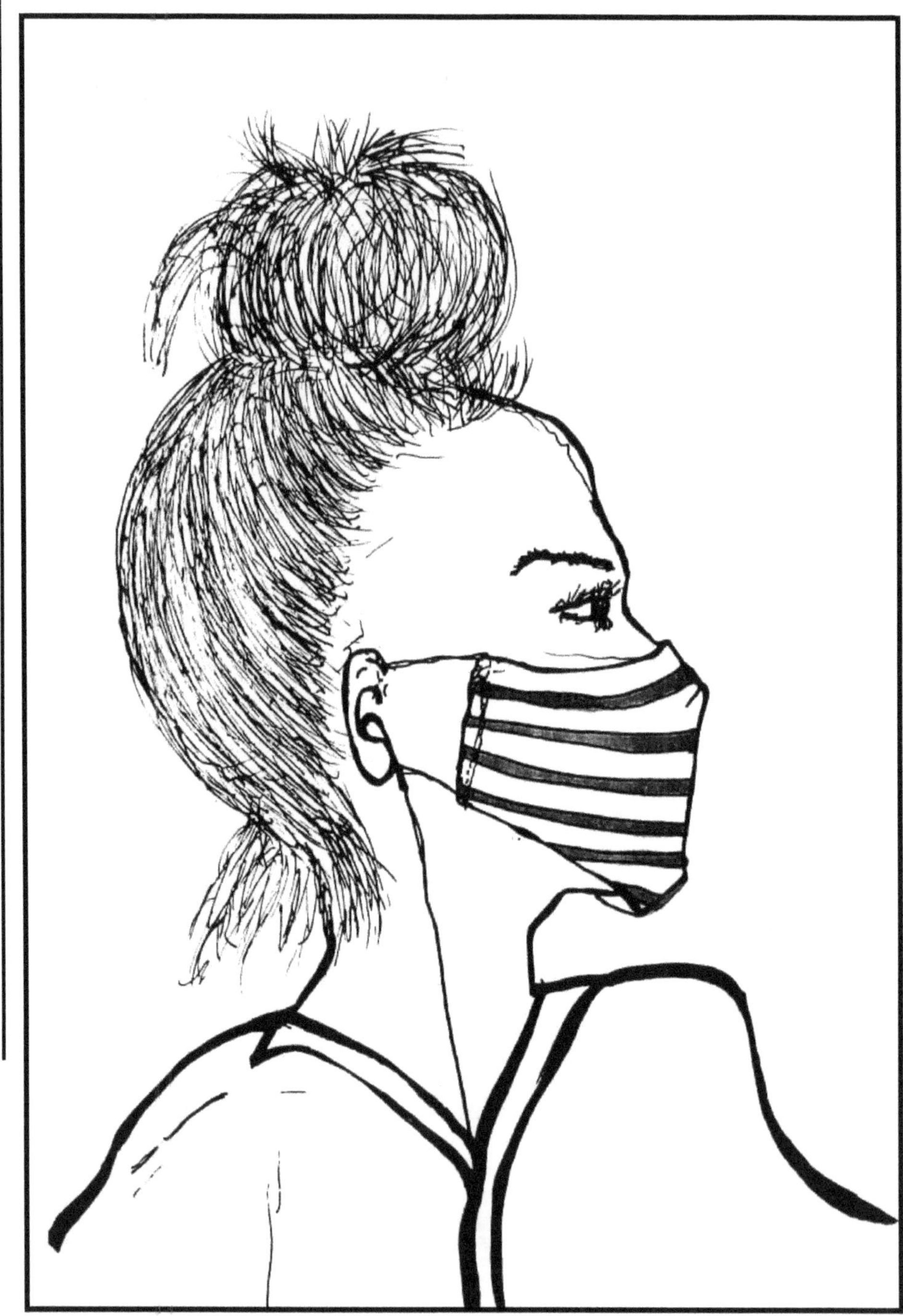

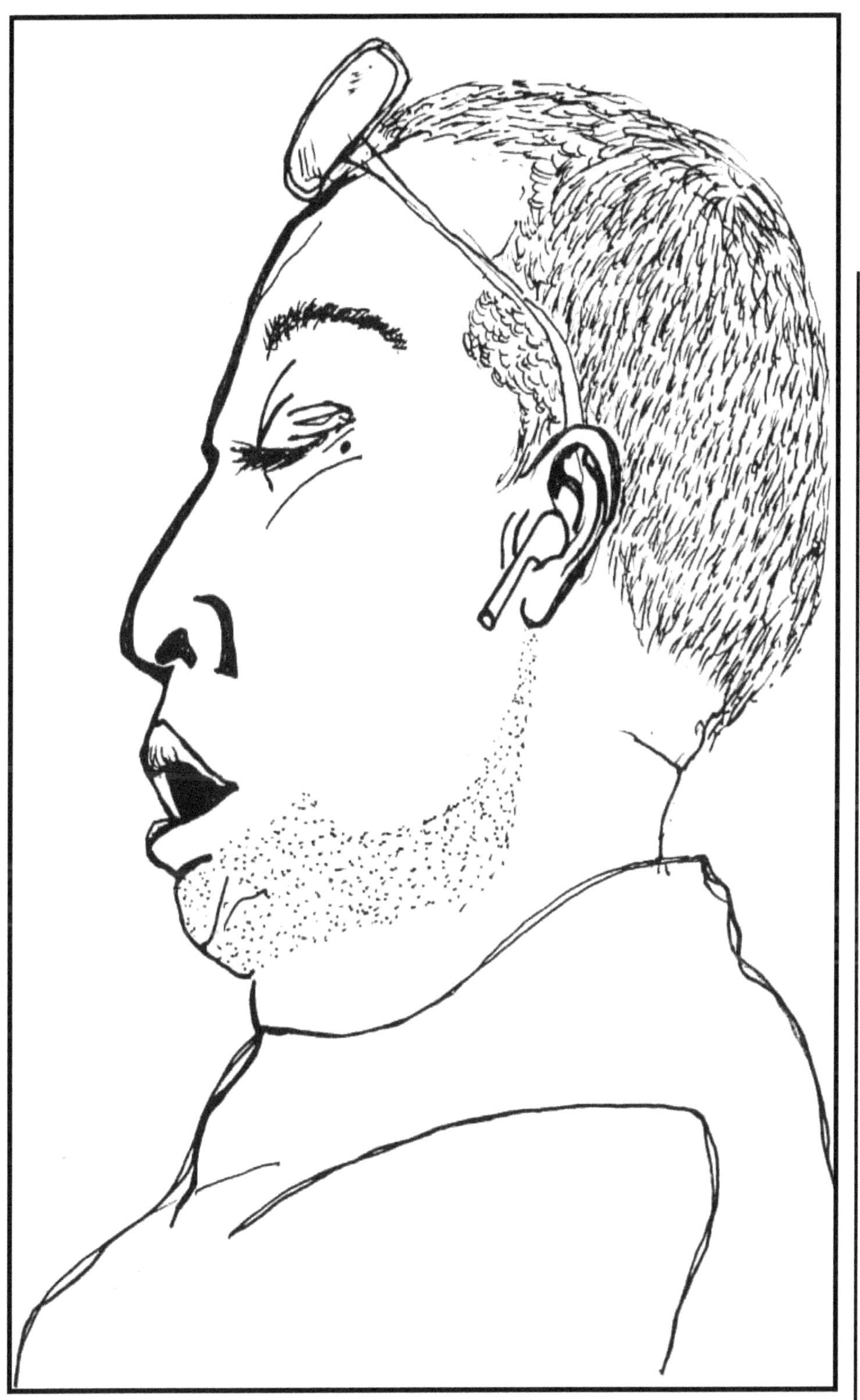

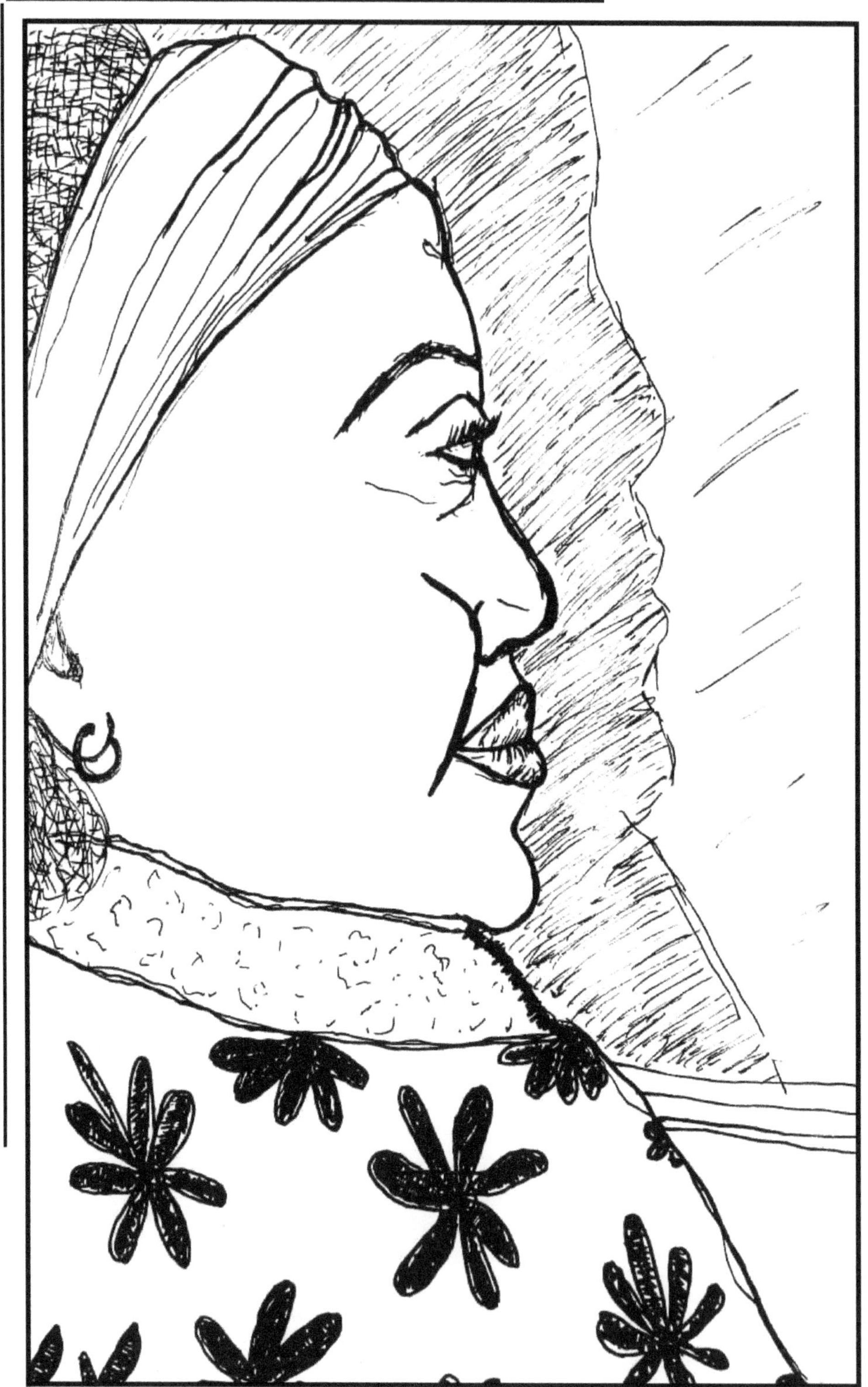

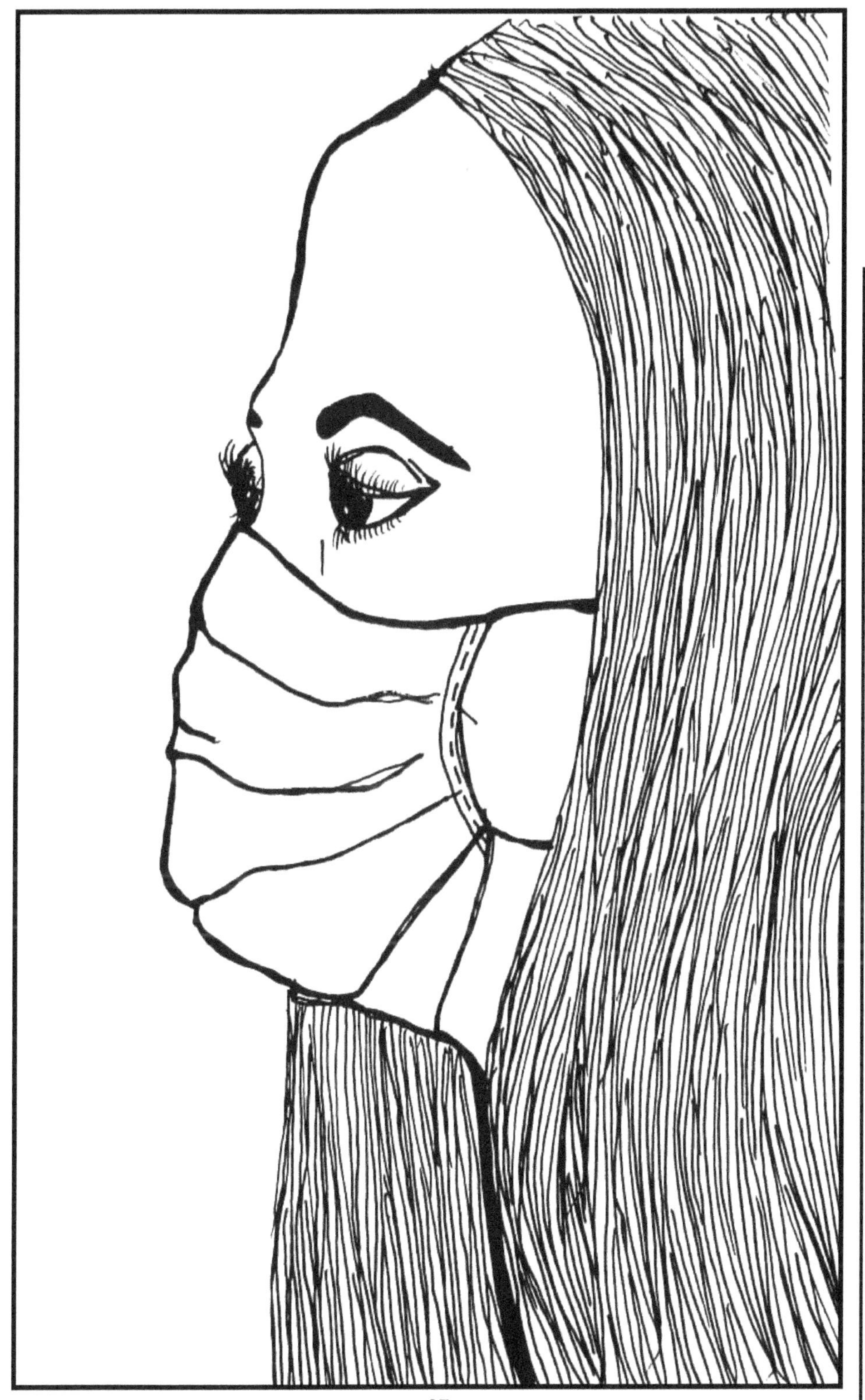

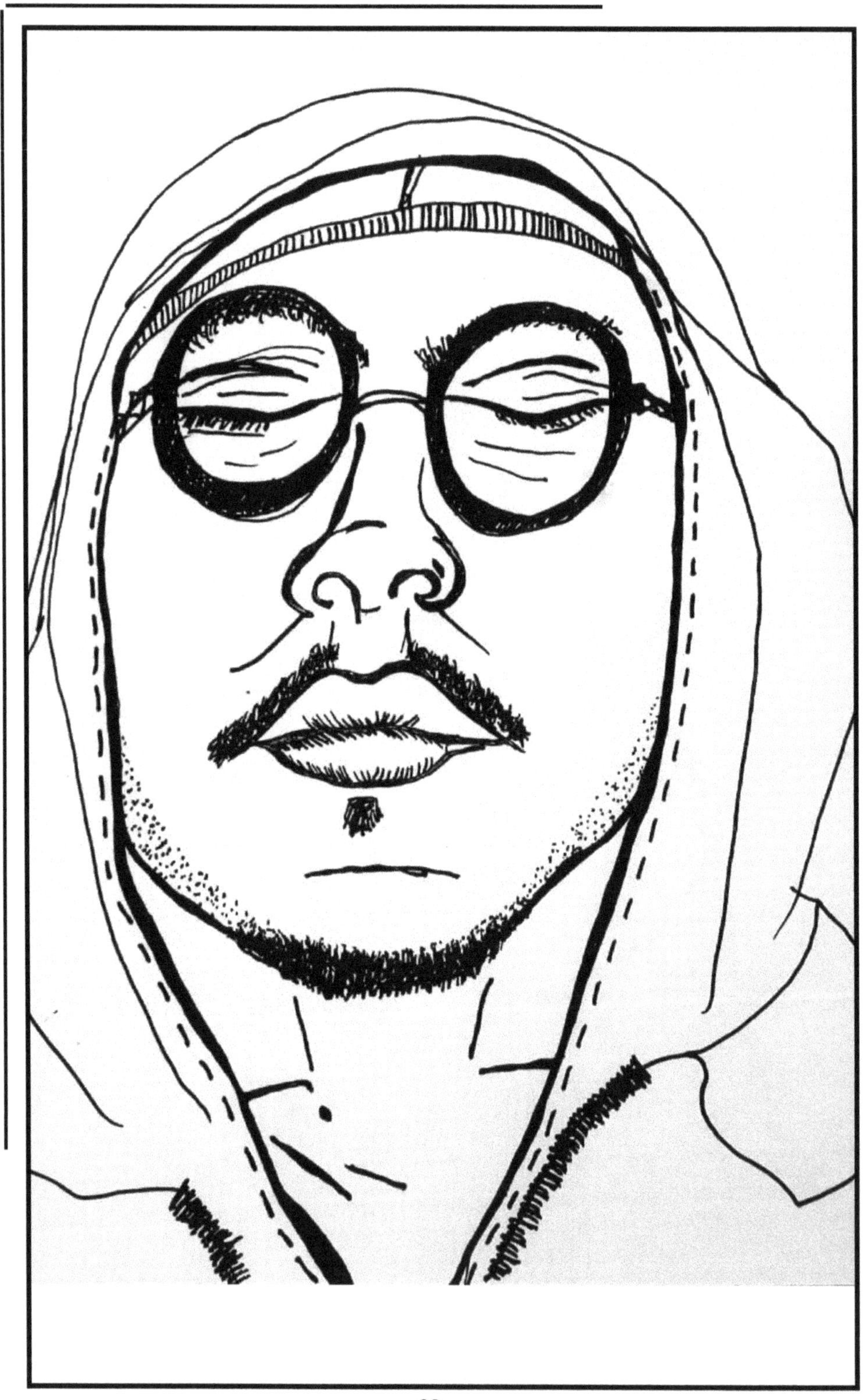

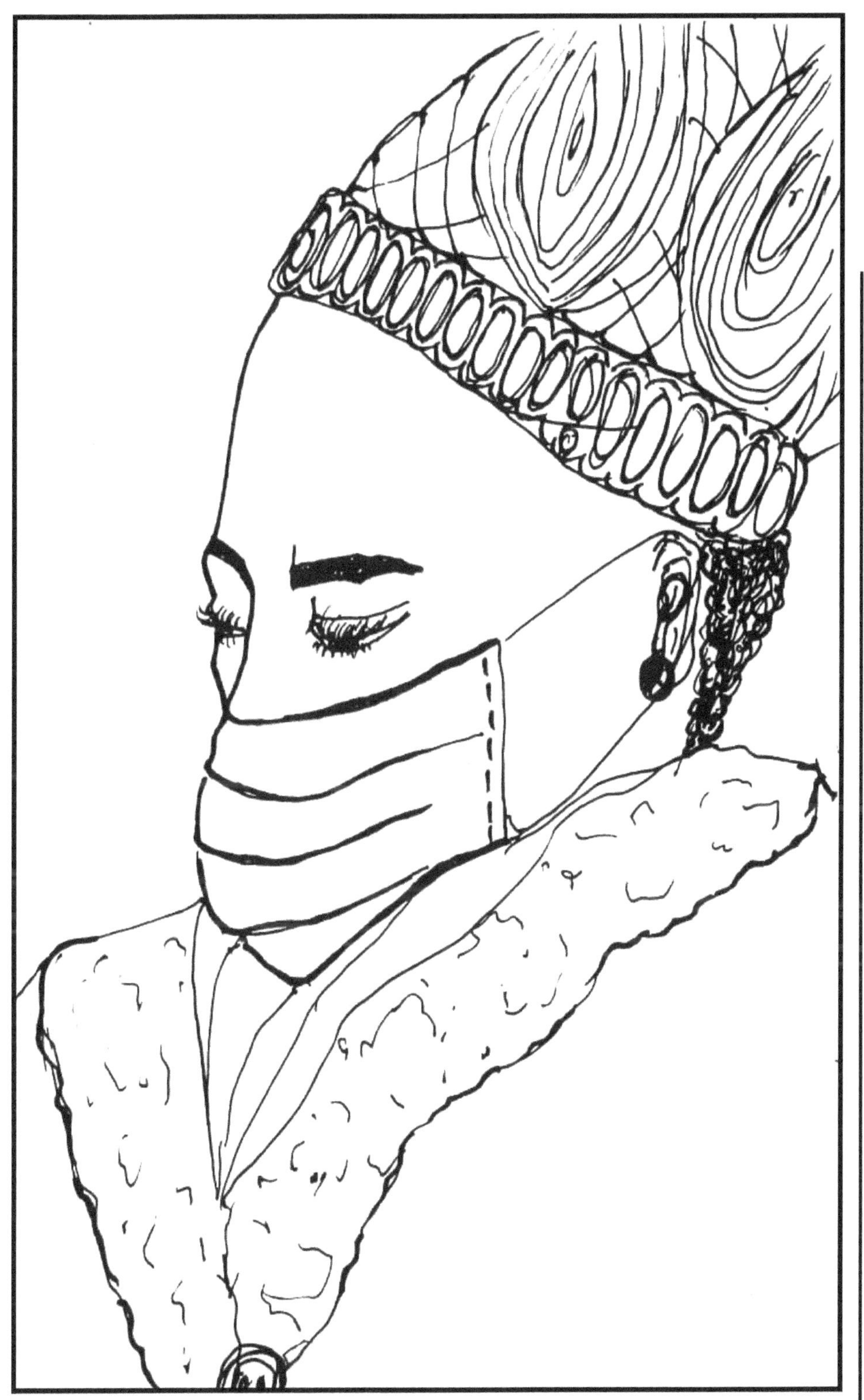

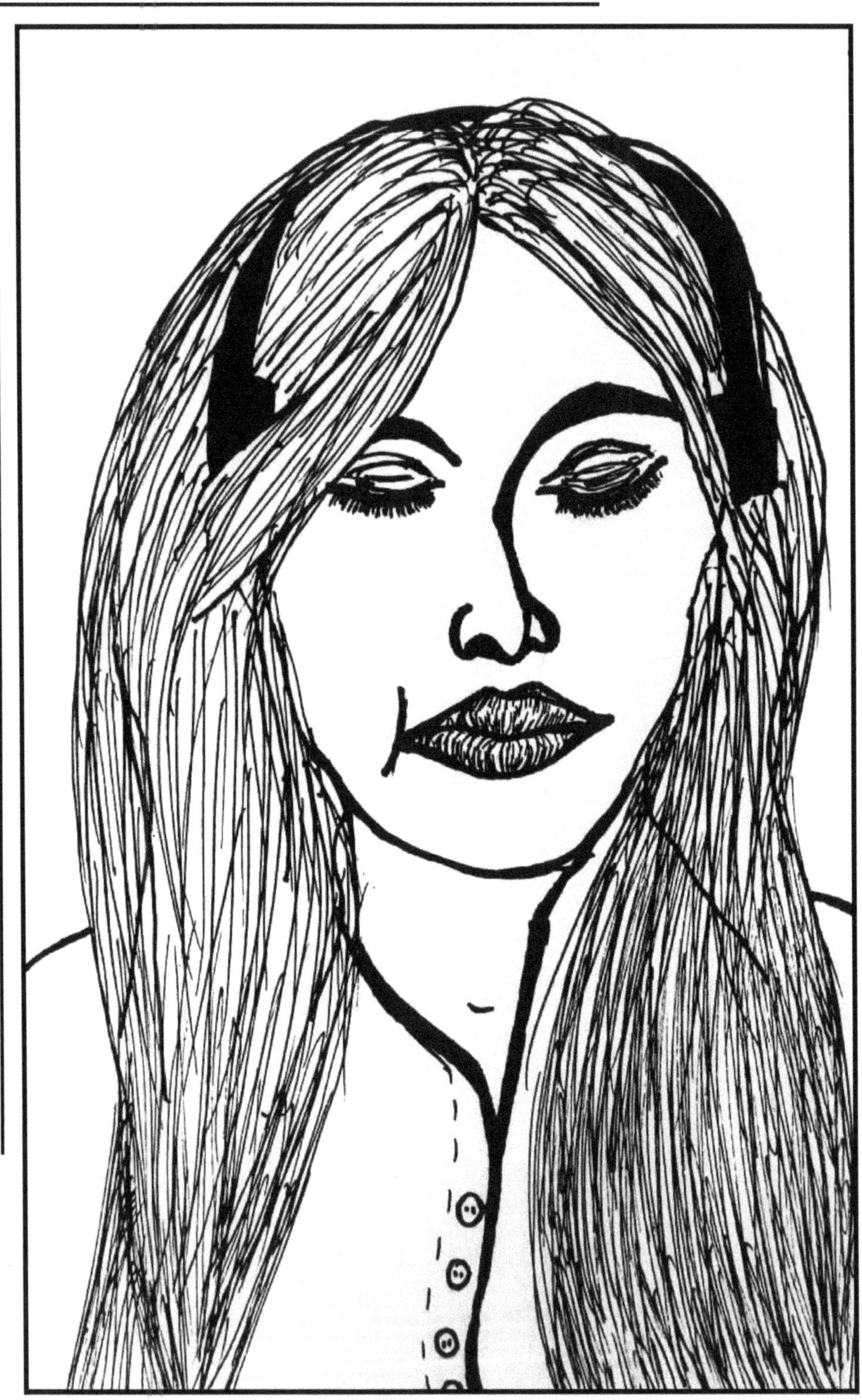

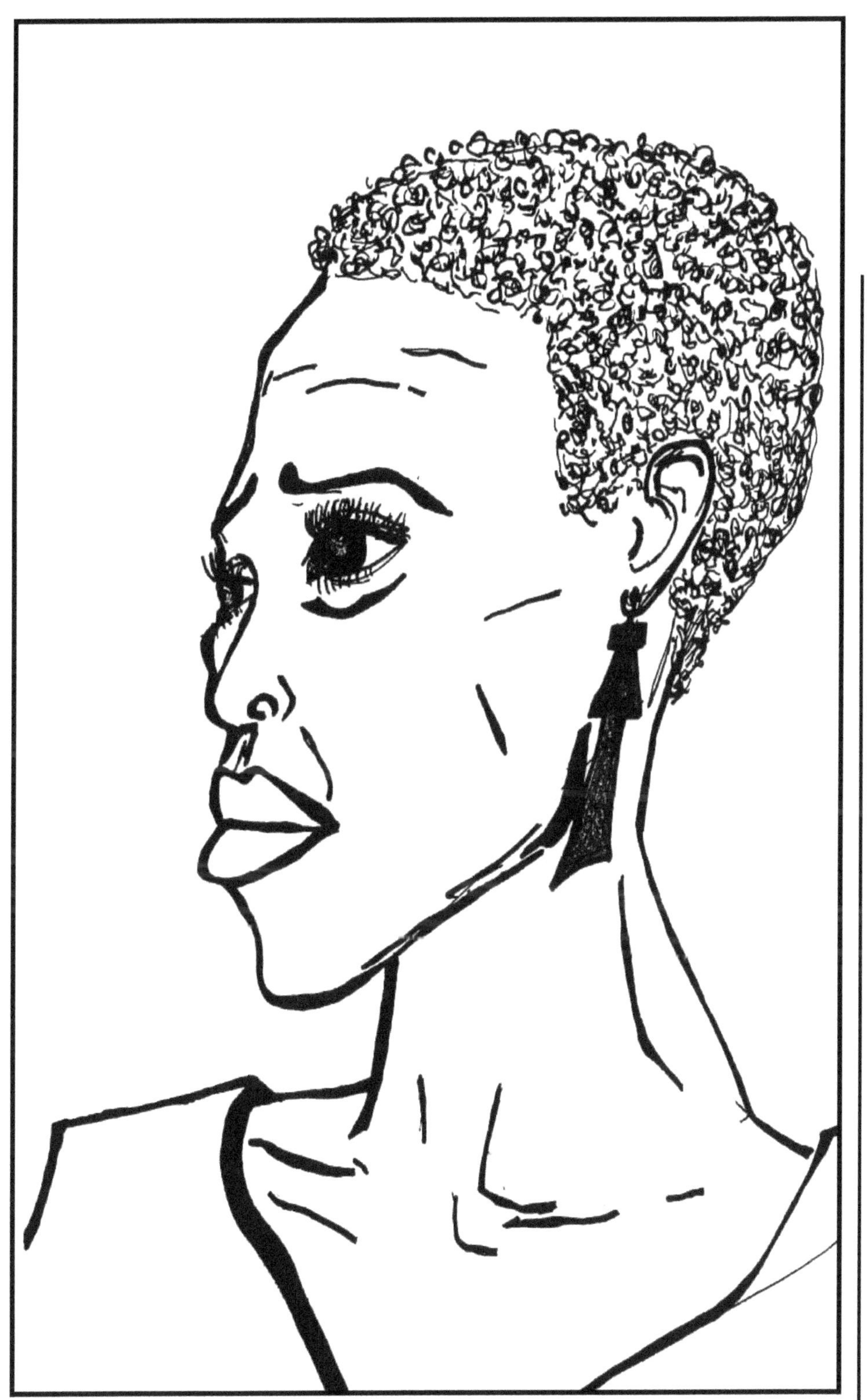

QAnon Reveals the True Identities of the Lindbergh Baby

Justin Neff

QAnon has successfully proven that JFK Jr. is alive and well in Pittsburgh. Now they reveal the eight people who are the missing Lindbergh baby, each fighting tirelessly to keep this country out of the hands of liberals and other losers.

Meryl Streep: We all should have seen this one coming. When asked point blank if she is in fact the son of the famed aviator Charles Lindbergh, Ms. Streep was speechless, only proving she knows exactly who she is. Her support of equal pay is only a cover story; her real goal is to reinstate isolationist policy and imprison anyone who mistakes her for Glenn Close.

Mitch McConnell: Again, not surprising once the facts are laid on the table. Mr. McConnell does a lesser job concealing his true identity than Ms. Streep. Not only does he still sleep in a crib and take a bottle every night, he supports the same ideals as his father, feeling whites are better than blacks at flying, building, and riding in airplanes.

Kirk Cameron: Go back and watch Growing Pains and then find a picture of Kirk Cameron today. The man/former baby does not age. Firmly in line with those who want to save this country from destruction, Mr. Cameron hosts a parenting and marriage podcast. For a reasonable fee, he'll also have a one-on-one Skype session. (For cybersecurity reasons, this former Lindbergh Baby does not do Zoom.)

Herschel Walker: Mr. Walker kidnapped himself from his crib at the age of 20 months and spent decades perfecting his glutes and traps for a career in the NFL. Though his on field accomplishments are endless, his main objective has been to prove Trump likes him because he's black, not because he's rich and famous.

Vincent Fusca (aka: JFK Jr.): There is no better cover than getting kidnapped from your crib, becoming JFK Jr., dying in a plane crash, then coming back to life as Vincent Fusca of Pittsburgh, PA. Though exposed, Mr. Fusca will remain living under the cover of both his pseudonym and a fedora.

Your daughter's friend, Eleanor (or Tessa/Olivia/Arianna) from daycare: Have you noticed her mom has been pretty pushy with getting a playdate going at the park, especially with social distancing and everything still going on? She's trying to hide right out in plain sight. Sorry, not sorry. Thanks to QAnon, little Eleanor's motive is clear as day: Make the Second Amendment the only Amendment.

Ellen: Don't think for one minute her fall from grace isn't a delicately designed ploy. Her perfect cover story, with the dancing, and surprises, and remaining married to Portia de Rossi even after the face surgery, had become a bit too perfect. Ellen's next step is to 'cancel' everyone who accepted her for being gay, and will out Nemo for being against the fishing industry. Very Lindbergh of her.

You: Go ahead and prove to the internet you are not the Lindbergh Baby. Were you once a baby? Are you now not a baby? Boom. Hard evidence. This does not mean your entire life has been a lie; it just means your family and friends and everyone around you is a big fucking liar. You need to join the 'Q'; it's the only way to save this country from the crazies.

Gender Reveal Party Conventions From Across The Ages

Rosalind Moran

The Big Bang Era: I am dust. What is dust? Should we try distinguishing dust from other dust? How can I tell which of you newly-formed dust pockets is Karen? Does anyone have a pink headband?

Vertebrates-Transition-To-Land-Based-Amphibians Era: Hatch aquatic egg. Watch egg crack open. Gender revealed.

Mammals-Develop-Opposable-Thumbs Era: Thumbs up for boy! Thumbs up for girl! Thumbs up for grasping branches! Yay thumbs!

Stone Age: Gender less interesting than using stone tools to draw rhinos on rocks. Have you seen this high-tech chip of granite I'm holding? Praise be to Rock God. I love stone chip.

Iron Age Cold Epoch: Ignore gender of naked infant and instead swaddle them immediately in leather and fur. What kind of rock-wit would reveal a baby's sex in this weather? Keep up, caveman!

Cradles of Civilisation Circa Bronze Age: Writing has been developed in South America, Africa, East Asia and the Middle East. Cradles everywhere are adorned with meaningful squiggles. A now-infamous Mesopotamian squiggler living in my cousin's basement has the bright idea of selling inflated goat bladder balloons that spell out 'boy' and 'girl' in cuneiform. The damage is done.

Meanwhile-In-Europe Era: Nobody can squiggle especially well, but a vague and misplaced sense of superiority reigns here nonetheless. Some of us more entrepreneurial pagans come up with colour-coded flower crowns for use in local gender reveals. Apparently this innovation – though destined to fall out of fashion for several thousand seasons – will experience a surprise revival in the 2010s. Yes, thank you; you're welcome; oh, you're too kind! But really, don't worship me – worship Nature.

Ancient Rome: For my gender reveal party, I will gather all my wealthiest friends in a small amphitheatre and flourish a single square of paper in the air. If the baby's a boy, the square is a ballot paper. If the baby's a girl, it's a napkin. Something tells me this symbolic demarcation of gender roles will stand the test of time.

Ancient China: To help make our gender reveals memorable, we developed the earliest known form of the modern piñata. If the baby's a girl, fill it with red or pink silks for luck. If it's a boy, fill it with red or pink silks as well – but make the piñata bigger! And in the shape of a dragon! Does anyone have any extra clay to make this piñata truly the greatest piñata anyone has ever seen? Ahem – anyway, the gender is revealed by the shape and size of the piñata, not the colours inside. I mean, colours to depict gender? What kind of a fool does that?

Pompeii's Golden Era: Our gender reveals are explosive! Step 1: Sculpt a volcano from plaster or clay around a small glass amphora. Step 2: Place some soda ash in the amphora along with a few drops of either pink or blue dye, depending on the sex of your baby. Step 3: After your guests have arrived, ask everyone to gather around and watch as you add some long-expired wine. The erupting bubbles will be either pink or blue. Of course, the soda ash usually has some rather noxious contaminants and everyone has to evacuate lest they breathe in too many strange gases and die, but it makes for a good show. Gender revealed!

New Testament Era: Virgin pregnancies are all the rage. Gender is typically revealed by a visiting angel.

Byzantine Empire: Our gender reveals are very traditional. For announcing a boy, enter a chariot race. As your horses lap the hippodrome of Constantinople, empty buckets of dyed blue sand from your chariot to billow in your wake. As for announcing a girl, simply walk around the outside of the hippodrome with your friends and say "Guess which little peanut won't be permitted to participate in chariot races because of their gender? Yep, that's right…!"

Lawless Era Of Pillage And Plunder: Was there a party to celebrate the child's impending arrival? Will I ever see the child, and will the child be allowed to play outside when they grow older? Then it's a boy!

The Dark Ages: Ours is an era of intellectual darkness between the fall of Rome and the Renaissance. Gender reveal parties are marked by all sorts of failures: accidentally sending an arrow through your father-in-law instead of the exploding confetti-filled target, for example; or painting your pet rat pink or blue and releasing it into the streets to proclaim your news, and unwittingly reviving the plague. Somewhere, someone secures a bow to the bald head of a biologically female baby. These are dark days.

The Middle Ages: For my baby's gender reveal, I will assemble my friends and have them watch with bated breath as I point to the object that represents my baby's sex and will travel with them throughout their life. If the baby is a boy, he will receive a pointy sword for stabbing heretics. If it's a girl, she will receive a pointy hat.

The Renaissance: We keep it subtle; classy; understated. Our gender reveal convention is simply that mothers announce their baby's sex through unveiling a specially commissioned 'Madonna and Child' portrait based on their own likeness. In such portraits, the mother's face will invariably look like a bored oval and their baby will probably bear a resemblance to a fat old man utterly done with looking rapturous. But as long as the painter remembers to paint the baby's genitals, the reveal is usually a success.

Natural Selection Primetime Era i.e. 1500s England: Gender reveal party time among the rich! Here we eat blue or pink treats depending on the sex of the child, and inevitably feel dreadfully ill afterwards. Yes, this plate is pewter – do you like it? Did you overeat again, Edwin?

Tudor Period: Gather all your nobles for a gender reveal. Cheer if it's a boy. Weep if it's a girl, and threaten a beheading. Escort the mother to safety as required.

1700s Era France: Bake a cake. Fill it with blue icing for a boy or pink icing for a girl. Tell people they can eat it but also refuse to give them any.

Victorian Era: If I'm having a girl, I'll gather all my friends together and simply hold up a little white dress! If I'm having a boy, on the other hand, I'll also gather all my friends together – and simply hold up a little white dress! In this time of anxiety and fear over societal degeneration, it's so nice there are still some traditional values to fall back on.

1940s Manufacturing Boom: New traditional values FOR SALE! Extra, extra, money money money HALF-PRICE NOW buy twice the number of clothes you need KA-CHING capitalism is god capitalism is god do I look happy yet REDUCED CLEARANCE SALE CLeaRAnCE cLeaRAnce SaLE rEDuced party party pink blue pink blue gender reveal blublupink balloons baloney binary binaaaarrrrrryyyyyyyy.... and I'll also buy the piñata with the pink filling. Do you have change for a $50?

Counterculture Era: Fuck capitalism and gendered clothing!

Capitalism-And-Gendered-Clothing-Resurge-As-Dominant-Culture Era: Someone tried telling me today that gendered clothing and gender reveals are reductionist. Mm-hmm, yah, I know. They were wearing an amazing headband though. Did I tell you we'll be shooting pink headbands out of a canon at our baby shower?

The-Mother-Of-The-Author-Is-Still-Dressing-The-Author Era: I will do my best to empower my daughter, encourage her to wear practical footwear, and eschew child-sized fishnet stockings. If anyone ever suggests she engages in a 'gender reveal', I will pepper spray them. Now why are all these clothes made of plastic?

Global Financial Crisis Era: Our gender reveals involve opening an envelope and revealing a quote for the projected amount of debt our child will accumulate in their quest to gain an education, find a job, and pay for healthcare and a place to live. All debt figures will be exorbitant, but if the unborn child is female, black, or both, their debt will be even greater! Don't forget to slide the quote back into the envelope and fry it on toast for dinner.

The 2010s: As the years grow warmer and consumptions spirals ever further out of control, those of us in the Western world turn to something we feel we can control: the cultural practice of holding a party to announce a child's gender based on their sex at birth. Of course, the joke is on us, seeing as we can neither dictate gender based on sex or even host a party without our colourful explosives igniting wildfires or occasionally killing the guests. But that aside, we've certainly come a long way since the time we used to worship Rock God, right? Right?

The Post-Anthropocene Era: I am dust. What is dust? Everything feels hot and grimy and I still can't distinguish dust from other dust. Fucking human progress, what an embarrassment. And I've lost my headband. Karen, where the hell are you?

Of Waves That End At Our Feet

Photography by Birdee
Poetry by Casey Riedel

At first my eyes were closed,
My lips drowned in constellations,
Hips swallowed,
In the heat of your legs.

Now,
Our bodies mesh in a never-ending rhythm,
My skin peels off in tiny squares
Raw from the constant friction.

My stomach spasms,
Thirsty for nutrients from our 24-hour bender.
It growls and roars, drunk on stomach acid,
Spitting out its digestive juice.

After the fourth day, I get a cold,
My flesh gasping for reprieve
As my sweat soaked body lubricates our desire,
Burning at a hellish temperature.

My bloated fingers burst,
Next, my swollen breasts sag
And my left foot dislocates from cramping.
Yet, we keep going.

Verging on animosity,
I snort a line of pheromones off his cheekbone.
My nostrils disintegrate and drip off my face.
"Are you close?"

I roll my eyes,
Exasperated,
When they bounce off his chest
And I'm left in the dark.

It's been twenty days,
My jaw so sore from
Chewing on the fat bone of lust,
And I'm still not finished.

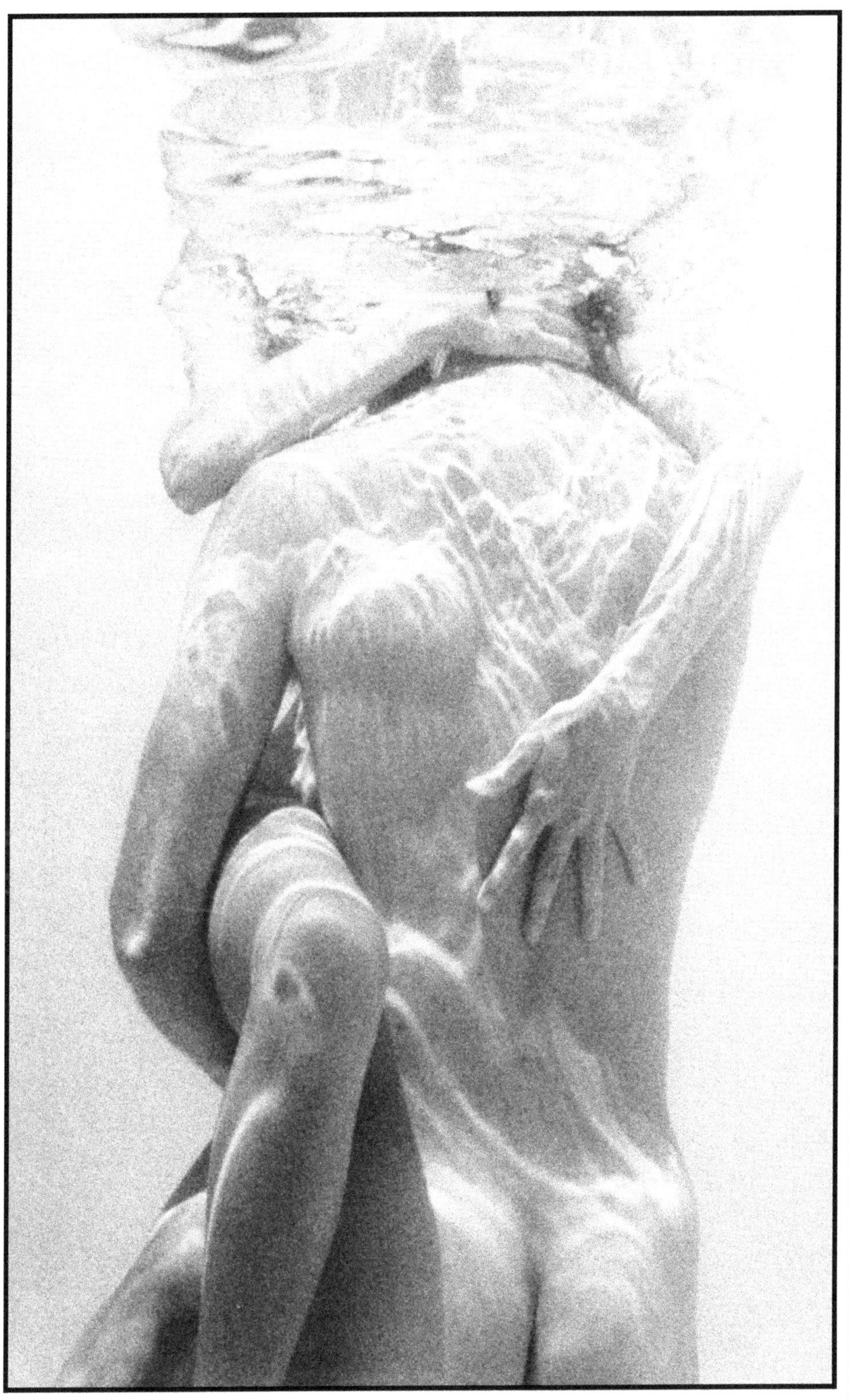

In Order Of Appearance:

Ed McManis is a writer, editor, erstwhile Head of School, and father—not always in that order. His work has appeared in more than 50 publications including Narrative, Blue Road Reader, Comstock Review, California Quarterly, & others. He, along with his wife, Linda, have just published esteemed author Joanne Greenberg's (I Never Promised You a Rose Garden) latest novel, Jubilee Year. He has two grown sons and two granddaughters.
Little known trivia fact: he holds the outdoor free-throw record at Camp Santa Maria: 67 in a row.
Flicker originally appeared in Unstamatic.

Miniature Malekpour is a current Ph.D. candidate at the Australian National University. She is currently a contributing writer for Diabolique Magazine. Twitter handle: @minamalekpour
Instagram handle: @malekpourminiature

Erica Hoffmeister is a wandering soul from Southern California who now lives in Denver, where she teaches college writing and advocates for media literacy and digital citizenship. She is the author of two poetry collections: Lived in Bars (Stubborn Mule Press, 2019), and Roots Grew Wild (Kingdoms in the Wild Press, 2019), but considers herself a cross-genre writer, with various works published in several journals and magazines. Learn more at: http://www.ericahoffmeister.com/.

Steph Butchko is a Brooklyn based visual artist and music producer. A graduate of NYU's Tisch School of the Arts Butchko creates under the pseudonym "Voir" - meaning to see. Butchko seeks to create works that play with perception while also investigating a human inclination towards spirituality. Illusian and scale are explored in order to expand the physical and mental relationship between viewer and art object.
Much of Butchko's inspiration can be found in the artist movements of the early 20th century as well as in the dogma of the Catholic Church. Iconography, worship and meditation are all subjects that inform Butchko's most recent works. IG: @voirhaus

Will Pewitt was born in Austin, TX and now lives in Jacksonville, FL where he teaches global literature. He publishes in a variety of genres, from fiction and poetry to history and philosophy. His other recent work includes translations of Arabic verse of the Abbasid era, which has appeared in Shenandoah. More of his writing can be found at WPewitt.com.

Dyslexic, former competitive weightlifter, J.B. Fredkin received BA degrees from Santa Clara University and an MFA from The New School creative writing program in New York. He has had his poetry published in: Pif Magazine, Atticus Review, Eunoia Review, Santa Clara Review, Best American Poetry Blog, and Belleville Park Pages. He currently lives, writes and teaches in San Francisco.

Charles Miller is a recent graduate of the University of Tennessee, but is a born and raised Texan. He is currently working an Americorps position in Northern Utah to gather 20,000 lbs of fruit to reduce food waste. He has been published in Caveat Lector, a publication of the Literary Society at UCD, and in Epoque Press, a UK ezine.
@charles_mayne

Paula Camacho is a Colombian-born painter and installation artist based in Orlando, Florida. She graduated from the University of Central Florida in the Fall of 2019 with her Bachelor of Fine Arts in Painting. Drawing from the profound teachings of Taoist philosophy, Paula's two and three-dimensional work aims to exemplify the transcendence of nature, and harmonize the duality of existence. She has participated in numerous exhibitions throughout Florida and has also exhibited work in New York City and Laguna Beach, California. Throughout July of 2019, Paula spent time as an artist in residence at the New York Academy of Art.
@paulacamacho.art

Josalyn Switzer is a student at the University of Nebraska at Omaha. She studies Creative Writing with concentrations in Creative Nonfiction and Poetry. She wants to go to graduate school for a Masters in Library and Information Science, and her dream is for her writing to help others feel less alone. Instagram: @josalynswitzer

Yeonjae (Jeannie) Eom is a creative writer who was born in Seoul, South Korea. She spent the bulk of her childhood predominately growing up in five different countries, all while she was traveling and experiencing twenty-seven other countries across the globe. Her experiences interacting with the world reflect on the writing she produces, shedding light on what is hidden in the darkness and bringing the buried perspectives to the forefront of critical discourse. Yeonjae (Jeannie) Eom is a previously published author of the book 'One World' which is now printed in both English and Korean, and she has published poetry titles across numerous magazines and award publications over international regions. Particularly, her work is majorly highlighted in American, Canadian, and Korean media, along with a handful of prestigious award publications in the Middle East. She is a current student at Phillips Exeter Academy in Exeter, New Hampshire, and she continues to explore and expand the realms of creative writing as she completes another publication of an upcoming book. Instagram @jeannie.com

Since beginning his Fine Arts education, Chris has remained a dedicated creative professional. After completing his foundation at Kootenay School of Art in Nelson, BC, he transferred to Alberta College of Art and Design in Calgary where he earned his BFA in 2001, majoring in Ceramics and Drawing. In 2004, Chris was selected for a residency at "The Pottery Workshop" in Shanghai China. During his (2 year) residency, he participated in group and solo exhibitions around China and Hong Kong. Upon request of the director his residency was extended, and he was asked to facilitate the startup of an international studio and residency in Jingdezhen China.
Jingdezhen is known as the historic birthplace of porcelain, which is still the major industry in this provincial city. There Chris studied numerous techniques from local craftspeople and artisans and began using Chinese brush painting to sketch and decorate his work.
After a disastrous solo exhibition in Hong Kong where 90% of his work arrived damaged, Chris abandoned ceramics to follow a new path in the creative industry. In 2008, he exhibited a collection of paper cut works based on traditional Chinese Folk Art. While the show was well received, it marked a turning point in his career where he became immersed in the emerging Fashion Design scene in Shanghai.
From 2009 to 2018 Chris directed his focus into designing textiles, graphics, and providing creative direction for the Shanghai based designer brand, HELEN LEE. The brand rose quickly to established itself as a leader in China's contemporary fashion and is frequently featured in international fashion publications receiving the "2013 Best Designer Award" from ELLE China. Chris's work, particularly in textile design, contributed greatly to the visual identity of the HELEN LEE brand and provided opportunities to create patterns and designs for well-known clients like Disney, Universal studios, Chivas, and IBIS Hotel group. Chris also currently designs Ski/Surf wear and prints for the athleisure brand "Perfect Moment" based in London, U.K.
After 18 years of living and working in China, Chris has relocated to his hometown Vancouver B.C. His passion to create by hand and urge to express himself artistically was reinvigorated when he opened his East Van studio in early 2020. His current work culminates his experience and developed style to create this recent body of work.
Instagram: @crkrtk

Andrew Last is high school mathematics teacher. In his spare time, he writes poetry and short stories. He recently became a father.

Greg Turlock is a published poet, author and photographer. His credits include "Rivers of Life", award-winning poem from the 2019 Alberta Arts Awards, "Hightops in the Snow", his new young-adult novel, "Prairie Survivors" photo essay in High Shelf Press, cover photo for the Parkland Poets II Anthology and "Beauty from the Underworld" photo and poem in Tiny Seed Journal. Greg lives in Parkland County, Alberta CANADA www.gregturlockcreative.com

Edward O. Byrne is an aspiring writer based in Western New York. He previously studied creative writing at Bard College in the Hudson Valley and after a period of mostly writing to and for himself, he has begun to focus on sharing his work more broadly.

MIKE PEREZ earned an M.A. in Creative Writing from FSU and an MFA from The University of Houston. His dad was an aviation expert and his mother is the poet Nola Perez -- thus Mike considers his current occupation as a professor at Embry-Riddle Aeronautical University to be merely Kismet (and DNA) fulfillment. His poems have been published or are forthcoming in GLASS, Bloom, Crab Orchard Review, Route Seven Review, Oscilloscope Lit Mag, Beyond Queer Words, Bangalore Review, The Journal of Florida Studies, Bluing The Blade, The Florida Journal, and at winningwriters.com as a finalist for their annual War Poetry Contest. Book chapters have appeared recently or are forthcoming in The Susan Sontag Anthology, Queer /Adaptations, The Power of Makeup, Beyond Binaries, and Essays On Billie Holiday, an anthology for which he also was lead editor.

Cynthia Yatchman is a Seattle based artist and art instructor. With an M.A. in child development and a B. A. in education, she has a strong interest in art education and teaches art to adults, children and families in Seattle. A former ceramicist, she studied with J.T. Abernathy in Ann Arbor, MI. though after receiving her B.F.A. in painting from the University of Washington she switched from 3D art to 2D and has stayed there since, working primarily on paintings, prints and collages. Her art is housed in numerous public and private collections and has been shown nationally in California, Connecticut, New York, Indiana, Michigan, Oregon and Wyoming. She has exhibited extensively in the Northwest, including shows at Seattle University, Seattle Pacific University, Shoreline Community College, the Tacoma and Seattle Convention Centers and the Pacific Science Center. She is an afOiliate member of Gallery 110 and is a member of the Seattle Print Art Association and COCA (Center of Contemporary Art)

Nava Derakhshani is a multimedia artist born to Iranian parents in Eswatini, Africa. She studied architecture at the University of Cape Town and worked in South Africa and India on low-cost eco-housing and urban design. Her Masters in Sustainable Development used photography and oral history to research spiritual ties to sustainable farming in Ethiopia. Based in New York, she works in ink and paper, ceramics, photography, moving image, and collage.

Justin Neff is a middle-aged dad who knows all the words to Frozen, Frozen II, and Olaf's Christmas Adventure. He used to know other things, too.

Rosalind Moran is a writer of fiction, non-fiction, reviews, poetry, and satire. Her work has been published by Prospect Magazine, Meanjin, Overland, The Lifted Brow, and Kill Your Darlings, among others. She received a Highly Commended in the 2019 June Shenfield Poetry Award and is a co-founder of Cicerone Journal. Twitter: @RosalindCMoran Instagram: @rosalindmoran

Since 2014, Jamie Johnson (Birdee) has been capturing the female form through her photography. In her work she examines themes of femininity, strength, and grace, as well as exploring the healing element of water. Her journey began with self portraiture as a means of embodiment and empowerment, and has since shared that same experience with others through immersive portrait sessions and fine art imagery.

Casey Riedel is a Creative Writing Major currently pursuing her dream of publishing a novel. She's an avid reader and writer with strong ties in grotesque poetry. @caykee_

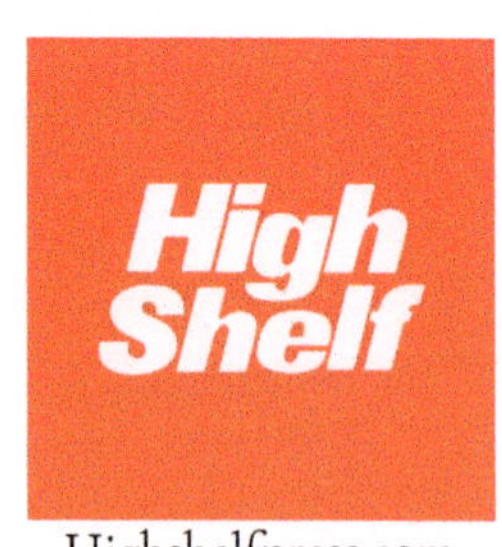

Highshelfpress.com